D1551315

The *Alt*Maine™ GUIDE

Your Alternative to the Usual Maine Tourist Guidebook

Second Edition

Dick Balkite
Jim Carter

*Alt*Maine
PUBLISHING

York Harbor, Maine

©2002 by Richard J. Balkite and James E. Carter

All rights reserved

No part of this book may be reproduced in any form, or by any electronic, mechanical or other means, without permission in writing from the publisher.

Published by AltMaine Publishing

York Harbor, ME 03911

w w w . a l t m a i n e . c o m

Cover design by Karen Brough

Book design by Karen Brough

The text of this book is set in Minion

Front cover photograph by Dan Gair

The AltMaine™ Guide / by Dick Balkite and Jim Carter

ISBN 0-9716050-0-9

Printed in Canada

Hignell Book Printing

Acknowledgements

This greatly expanded edition of The AltMaine Guide could not have been written without the knowledge and guidance of a goodly number of people. Some shared particular knowledge of a region; others, knowledge of a given interest area and still others helped us think through just how it should all come together.

So, thank you Bridget Coullon, John Dundas, Jeanne Gamage, Cynthia Hosmer, Sister Therese Pelletier, Dan Soule, Moira Smith, Helen Rollins, Woodrow Thompson and Jackie Villinski. And, special thanks to Irv Hodgkin who seemed to know everyone in Maine and who opened many doors for us.

Thanks also to everyone who wished us well and provided us with day-to-day encouragement.

And, of course, our thanks to all the individuals and organizations that work ceaselessly to protect, preserve and enhance the great state of Maine, our wonderful legacy.

Your Perfect Companion to
The AltMaine Guide

The AltMaine Map

Which routes to take and which to avoid

✦

Just where those "special places" are

✦

"Tours" for special interests

To order or learn more, just go to

w w w . a l t m a i n e . c o m

Contents

Contents

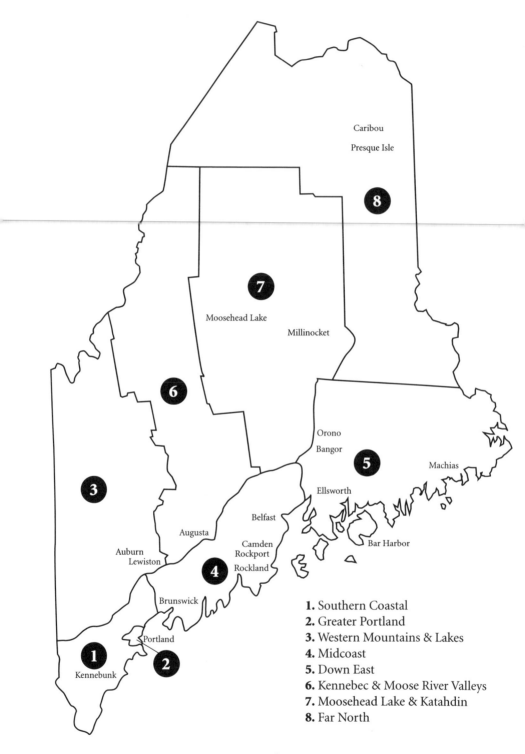

Caribou

Presque Isle

8

7

Moosehead Lake

Millinocket

6

Orono

Bangor

5

Machias

Ellsworth

Belfast

Augusta

Camden
Rockport

Auburn

3

Lewiston

Rockland

4

Bar Harbor

Brunswick

Portland

1

2

Kennebunk

1. Southern Coastal
2. Greater Portland
3. Western Mountains & Lakes
4. Midcoast
5. Down East
6. Kennebec & Moose River Valleys
7. Moosehead Lake & Katahdin
8. Far North

Introduction

"Not Many" in Kokadjo, by Dick Balkite

The AltMaine Guide is a unique guidebook.

We call it "AltMaine" because it's an alternative to the usual guidebook — written for the discerning visitor to a very special place. It's written for those who want to experience what makes this great state so special without having to endure the crowds, traffic and typical tourist attractions that can obscure the unique qualities of the real Maine.

This book also serves as a guide to those who not only appreciate all that Maine has to offer, but who would like to see it protected and preserved for future generations. Thus, you will see sections you won't see in other guidebooks. "Great Contributors to Maine," for example, briefly outlines the contributions made by 10 living Mainers who, often over a lifetime, have given greatly of their time, talent and energy to making this state the wonderful place it is. Another section, "Giving — the Maine Way," offers a number of suggestions on how you, too, can be a positive force in keeping Maine special for generations to come.

We want you to not only partake of and enjoy the treasure that is Maine, but to join us in our ongoing efforts to protect, preserve and even enhance it.

The AltMaine Guide also differs from other guidebooks in that it includes a highly selective listing of generally unknown and unpublicized destinations, events, accommodations and activities. The book is designed specifically for those who want to savor the uniqueness of Maine while avoiding mobs of tourists and the homogenized tourist attractions that discriminating visitors are trying to escape by coming to Maine in the first place.

Emphasis is on unspoiled and uncrowded attractions often missing from the usual guides — public gardens, summer chapels, farmers' markets, scenic views, wildlife reserves, theater, music, ecological preserves, art and antiques, natural habitat, craft fairs, old trains, festivals, spas, spiritual and health retreats, special educational opportunities and much more.

You'll also find carefully-screened and selected attractions that are listed in some other guides, but with suggestions on how to enjoy them without getting into the tourist mainstream — out-of-the-way, yet special inns, lodges and B&Bs, unspoiled campsites, museums, parks, exceptional restaurants, cruises, historic sites, beaches, ferries....

We've even added a section on Maine's ghosts, including their stories and where you might encounter them, should you desire. And no guide to Maine would be complete without the lighthouses, so we not only provided a complete listing of them, including their locations and descriptions, but included a section on their history, as well.

You'll find the largely-secret, such as an open chapel overlooking the sea (dedicated to families who have lost children) and special schools for learning boatbuilding, photographic skills or even how to document a person's life. You can even find a listing for a holistic healing festival.

AltMaine category listings are geographically organized so you can find and explore a variety of interesting and enjoyable attractions wherever you find yourself in any given region of the state. Wherever possible, listings include phone numbers, websites and email addresses to provide you with easy access to additional information.

So don't worry about the crowds, the traffic, the T-shirt shops and the tourist traps — come and enjoy the real Maine...the way life should be.

And join us as we endeavor to keep it that way.

Antique Shows & Auctions
(Special events for antique lovers)

Photo by Dick Balkite

Antiques can be found in every corner of Maine; you need no guide to help you find dealers and retail shops. There are, however, several events, some sponsored by the Maine Antiques Dealers Association and similar organizations that are of particular interest to those who take their antiques seriously.

The Annual Antiques Show — July — Portland
The Racquet and Fitness Club, 2445 Congress Street
(207) 882-4255 or (207) 883-3443
www.maineantiques.org/events.html

Antiques Coastal Maine — August — Damariscotta
Round Top Center for the Arts, Business Route 1
(207) 882-7908
www.maineantiques.org/events.html

Decoy Auction — July — Cape Neddick
The Cliff House, Shore Road
Swap, sell and buy — over 800 investment-quality decoys and related items.
(207) 778-6256
www.guyetteandschmidt.com

American and European Art Auction — August — Portland
Barridoff Galleries, PO Box 9715
Portland, ME 04104
(207) 772-5011
www.barridoff.com
email: fineart@barridoff.com

Maine Antiques Festival — August — Union
At the Fairgrounds
(207) 563-1013
www.mainantiquefest.com
email: cpishows@lincoln.midcoast.com

Bath Antiques Shows
A series of shows throughout the year at various locations in and around Bath.
email: ptpromo@suscom-maine.net

Biking
(Scenic trails at just the right speed)

Biking in Acadia National Park, courtesy of Maine DOT

No matter how you travel in Maine you have a sense of just how great a place it is. However, if you truly want to savor Maine and still cover a fair bit of distance, nothing beats travel by bike. Biking lets you stop whenever you want to chat with people along your route — the best way to meet the locals and find out what's special in the area. Also, its easy to divert to back roads, stop and go for a hike, set up camp, stay in a B&B, sample roadside fare, watch a moose, take in a fair or just savor the moment — all with a minimum of fuss. Biking also gets you out in the air and sunlight (full disclosure requires us to say we sometimes have rainy days) and gives you a great sense of being alive in one of the most wonderful places to be alive.

The Maine Department of Transportation (MDOT) originally compiled the tours described in this section. They did so in conjunction with experienced Maine cyclists and leading state cycling organizations. If a tour in this section appeals to you, please get more details. Simply go to www.exploremaine.org/bike, select the tour that interests you and download the exact directions, tips, cautions, etc. Another option is to call the MDOT at (207) 287-6600 or email them at john.balicki@state.me.us. In addition to the tour information you should have a very good local map. We recommend the Maine Atlas and Gazetteer from DeLorme Mapping Co. (www.delorme.com). When you decide on your tour, be sure to check other sections of The AltMaine Guide to find out what other interests you might explore along your route.

If you're interested in a full schedule of rides, races and other events throughout the year, all over Maine, check in with the Bicycle Coalition of Maine. Their address is PO Box 5275, Augusta, ME 04332, or on the web at www.BikeMaine.org.

Wheel on to great new adventures.

S o u t h e r n   C o a s t a l

• *South Coast Tour — 50 Miles of Flat Terrain*
Beautiful beaches and historic towns with art galleries and museums characterize this tour. Takes you past Walkers Point and the summer home of former President George Bush. Many other gorgeous summer "cottages." During the warm months, slip off for some sun worshipping. Starts in Wells, to Kennebunk, Kennebunkport, Biddeford Pool looping back to Kennebunk and Wells. Road conditions are good but no shoulders.

G r e a t e r   P o r t l a n d

• *Portland Lighthouses Tour — 43 Miles of Flat Terrain*
Takes you through the working waterfront with boats and ships of every kind. In the Old Port stop to savor the wonderful restaurants and unique shops. Several lighthouses, state parks, beaches, a narrow gauge railway, salt marshes and wonderful views of Casco Bay and the Atlantic. Starts in Portland, looping through Scarborough and Cape Elizabeth, back to Portland. Good road conditions, some wide paved shoulders. Moderate to heavy traffic entire route.

W e s t e r n   M o u n t a i n s   &   L a k e s

• *Western Foothills Tour — 60 Miles of Flat to Very Hilly Terrain*
A step back in New England time to hilly country roads, stone walls, maple lined streets, river views and a covered bridge. Starts in Cornish, then to Hiram, Brownfield, Kezar Falls, Parsonfield, Newfield, Limerick then back to Cornish. Generally good road conditions with some narrow, winding roads and blind hills. Traffic is light except near Cornish.

• *Lake Auburn Tour — 35 Miles of Rolling Terrain*
Constantly-changing terrain with views of mountains near and far as well as lakes. Starts in Auburn to West Minot, Hebron, Turner and back to Auburn along

Lake Auburn. Road conditions fair with lots of narrow, winding roads with blind hills. Traffic ranges from light to moderate, occasionally heavy.

• *Franklin County Heritage Tour — 110 Miles of Rolling Terrain*
Perfect multi-day tour to allow side trips and explorations. Mountains and lakes combined with a wide variety of museums and historical societies along the way. Starts in the university town of Farmington, to Strong, Phillips, Rangeley, Kingfield, then back to Strong and Farmington. Mostly light traffic but possibly heavy near Farmington. Limited services along the tour so be prepared with water, food, first aid kit, warm clothes, spare parts and repair tools.

• *Evans Notch Tour — 73 Miles of Hilly to Mountainous Terrain*
Challenging multi-day ride with views of three mountain ranges. Two long climbs. Slips you over the border into neighboring New Hampshire. Begins in the ski capital of Bethel, south to Lovell, looping north on Rt. 113, then east on Rt. 2 back to Bethel along the Androscoggin River. Mostly narrow roads with no shoulders and some broken pavement. Mostly light traffic.

• *Grafton Notch Tour — 74 Miles of Mountainous Terrain — Flat Along River*
Challenging multi-day ride with many hiking options. Combines scenic treasures and a covered bridge with a good chance of a moose sighting. Begins in Rumford, looping south, then north to Upton, Newry, then back to Rumford. Road conditions are generally fair with some broken pavement. Limited services along the tour so be prepared with water, food, first aid kit, warm clothes, spare parts and repair tools.

Midcoast

• *Waldo County Ridge Tour — 70 Miles of Flat to Rolling Terrain*
This is a quiet, rural tour with great views, farms and old barns. Begins on the coast in Belfast, generally north and west toward Brooks, south and west to Liberty, north and east to Searsmont, then back to Belfast. Road conditions are generally fair with some broken pavement. Traffic is light to moderate.

• *Rockland & Port Clyde Tour — 51 Miles of Rolling Terrain*
Renaissance Rockland, museums, state parks, lighthouses and the picturesque village of Port Clyde. Begins in Rockland where you should try out one of the great new eateries, to Owls Head, South Thomaston, St. George, Tenants Harbor to Port Clyde. Then, up along the St. George River to Thomaston and back to Rockland. Road conditions are generally fair. Light traffic around Owls Head, otherwise fairly heavy urban traffic.

D o w n   E a s t

• *Passamaquoddy Bay Tour — 27 Miles of Moderate Grades*
Bay views, forests, farmland, lakes, birds and fish ladders. A great tour for beginner cyclists because of the good pavement, low traffic and moderate grades for a very doable distance. Starts in Pembroke, then a coastal loop back to Pembroke.

• *Penobscot County Tour — 92 Miles of Flat to Rolling Terrain*
The tour begins by following the Penobscot and Piscataquis Rivers, then swinging south through agricultural lands. Farms, rivers, dams and old mills— American industrial history. Begins in downtown Bangor, Old Town, Howland and back down to Bangor. Light traffic in the northern reaches, moderate to heavy near Bangor. There is one 20-mile stretch without services so be prepared with water, food, first aid kit, warm clothes, spare parts and repair tools.

• *Washington County Tour — 94 Miles of Flat to Rolling Terrain*
Coastline, forests and blueberry barrens — something for everyone. Begins in Machias, to East Machias, Dennysville, Lubec, Cutler and back to Machias. Mostly light traffic but expect 20 miles of unpaved shoulders and about 2 miles of gravel. Fat tires are recommended.

• *Schoodic Peninsula Tour — 29 Miles of Flat to Moderate Terrain*
Schoodic Head jutting out into the Atlantic, rolling surf and fishing villages. Begins in West Gouldsboro, to South Gouldsboro, Winter Harbor, around Schoodic Head in Acadia National Park, Prospect Harbor and back to West Gouldsboro. Road conditions generally good and traffic light to moderate.

• *Deer Isle-Stonington Tour — 31 Miles of Flat to Rolling Terrain — 3 Short Climbs*
Fishing villages, coves, beaches and lots of art and artists. Begins in Deer Isle, Stonington, Sunset, South Deer Isle and back to Deer Isle. Be prepared to spend a fair bit of time in Stonington, a working fishing village and once home to several quarries. Road conditions are fair, but they are narrow and without shoulders. This tour has approximately 0.5 miles of dirt road and fat tires are recommended. There are no basic services along this route so be prepared with water, food, first aid kit, warm clothes, spare parts and repair tools.

Kennebec & Moose River Valleys

• *Kennebec Valley Tour — 68 Miles of Very Hilly Terrain*
Hilly, scenic, river route Benedict Arnold took to assault Quebec during the Revolutionary War. Farms and mountains plus surprising Skowhegan. Begins in Skowhegan, to Athens and north to Rt. 16, west to Bingham, south to Solon and back to Skowhegan. Generally fair road conditions, some broken pavement, but light traffic throughout the tour.

• *Waterville-China Lake — 49 Miles of Hilly Terrain*
Challenging hills, lakes, ridge rides, great views and charming villages. Starts in Waterville, to North Vassalboro, China, Weeks Mills and back to Waterville. Generally good road conditions but one unpaved stretch of about one mile. Fat tires recommended. Also, there are no bicycle services along the route so be prepared with spare parts and repair tools.

Moosehead Lake & Katahdin

• *Penquis Tour — 55 Miles*
Mountains, lakes and rivers with vast woodlands and potato farms. A giant loop beginning in St. Albans, to Dexter, Dover-Foxcroft, Guilford and back to St. Albans. Generally good road conditions although some dirt sections and uneven surfaces. Fat tires recommended. Mostly light traffic with heavy traffic to and from Dover-Foxcroft.

• *Katahdin Area Tour — 60 Miles of Hilly Terrain with Major Climbs*
The Great North Woods. This tour has magnificent views of Mt. Katahdin and plenty of opportunities to spot wildlife. Begin in Island Falls, to Smyrna Falls, Sherman, Patten and back to Island Falls. Intermittent broken pavement so fat tires are recommended. There are no services for a 26-mile stretch so be prepared with water, food, first aid kit, warm clothes, spare parts and repair tools. Traffic is generally light, but allow the logging trucks plenty of room. For off-trail biking take Rt. 159 out of Patten to Baxter State Park. Bikes are allowed only on the gravel perimeter road.

Far North

• *St. John Valley Tour — 91 Miles of Rolling Terrain*
Maine's "Big Sky Country." This tour has small towns, agriculture and lots of Acadian culture. It's the most culturally distinct section of Maine. Starts at

Caribou, to St. Agatha, Lille, Van Buren (across from St. Leonard, New Brunswick) and back to Caribou. Road conditions generally good, some broken pavement on backroads. Traffic heavy near Caribou, moderate along the St. John River and light most other places. Give logging trucks plenty of room. Many opportunities for off-road biking.

• *Potato Country Tour — 50 Miles of Rolling Terrain*
    This tour takes you to the heart of Maine's rural agricultural landscape. This is the heart of Aroostook, Maine's largest county, usually referred to as "The County." Track the Aroostook River past potato fields and farms, the key to the region's economy. Starts in Presque Isle, to Washburn, Caribou, Fort Fairfield and back to Presque Isle. Road conditions are poor to fair. Be cautious of heavy traffic in Presque Isle and Caribou.

Birding — In Exceptional Places

Sun-bleached timbers on The Golden Road, by Dick Balkite

Maine affords opportunities for birding almost everywhere with mountain, woodland, marsh and seashore habitats. However, some places are just so unique that we had to create a special section for them. These sites will afford you opportunities few birders will ever have the chance to enjoy. You can see a wide variety of birds in truly exceptional environmental settings, far from the maddening crowds. Your companions will not only be birds, but a wider variety of wildlife, ranging from fox and moose to porpoise and whale. These exceptional locales range from deep within the Great North Woods to islands well out to sea. Viewing birds in these special places may require you to travel remote dirt roads, slip into a kayak or board a boat. You might even find yourself in a small plane. We expect that just getting to each site will be a memorable event in itself. Once you're there, revel in your happy circumstances and enjoy the birding.

Western Mountains & Lakes

• Brownfield Bog
Here's an opportunity to go birding by foot, or better yet by kayak or canoe. Brownfield Bog is officially known as the Brownfield Bog Wildlife Management Area. It's a 5,700-acre tract, not far from Fryeburg, owned and managed by the Maine Department of Inland Fisheries and Wildlife. It's an area bisected by the meandering Saco River enabling you to encounter areas of open water, shallow wetlands, seasonally-flooded woodlands, old fields and upland forests. It is covered primarily with dense aquatic vegetation with oaks and maples overhanging the wetlands. This is where you can find willow flycatchers, blue-gray gnatcatchers

and yellow-throated vireos. You will also likely spot several species of nesting waterfowl and a goodly number of wetland and woodland breeders. Bald eagles appear occasionally along with red-shouldered hawks.

While you're watching for all the birds, keep you eye out for other wildlife. The Brownfield Bog is known as home to moose, beaver, river otter, mink, muskrat and white-tailed deer.

From Fryeburg head south on Rts. 5/113. At the intersection of Rts.5/113 & 160 in East Brownfield, turn north onto Rt. 160. Continue 0.8 miles across the Saco River. Continue another 0.7 miles and take the left fork onto Lord Hill Rd. Go approximately 0.1 miles to a dirt road on the left with a sign for Brownfield Bog Wildlife Management Area. Follow the dirt road for 0.7 miles to the MDIFW building and parking area. Park here and begin your explorations on foot. You are right on the edge of the marsh so you can launch your kayak or canoe here also. Water travel will obviously enable you to more fully explore the river and wetland areas. If you travel by foot, boots are an excellent suggestion anytime of year. Regardless of how you travel, be sure to bring insect repellent.

More Info: Contact the Bridgton Lakes Information Center, PO Box 236, Bridgton, ME 04009 (207) 647-3472.

Midcoast

• *Matinicus Island & Matinicus Rock*

Matinicus Island is a bit of heaven 26 miles off the coast. It's a low-lying and isolated island about two miles long and about one mile wide, very rustic and very quiet. That's to be expected given a population of about 200-300 in summer and less than 100 in winter. It's a place where your entertainment comes from within because Matinicus is a fishing community, not a resort. Happily, it offers no golf course, tennis court, hotel, motel or public camping. There are, however, cottage rentals and at least one B&B.

The island is a botanist's delight and a bird lover's paradise. It is an ideal place for gathering wildflowers, ferns and berries. Over 650 species have been identified along the quiet woodland trails, rocky shores and flowering fields. Dense stands of spruce and fir dot the island especially on the eastern and western shores. The interior is more open with grassy fields and low, deciduous shrubs. There is also a cattail marsh on the northeast shore and a small freshwater pond in the interior. The shores are rocky, the eastern shore mostly granite, but there are two large beaches with grayish-white sand and numerous small pebble beaches.

Matinicus is on the spring and fall migratory path of many bird species and is perhaps the rival of Monhegan Island as a flyway stop. You just might spot gyrfalcon, redheaded woodpecker, scissor-tailed flycatcher, white-eyed and yellow-throated vireos, yellow-breasted chat, lark sparrow, dickcissel, orchard oriole and a host of other species. Also, keep you eye out for green heron in the pond area.

The truly adventurous might make the effort to reach Matinicus Rock, the lighthouse station only five miles to the south. It's a barren, wind-swept piece of granite rising only 60 feet from the sea. There you will find rare, nesting Atlantic puffin, Arctic tern and storm petrel. Boats are not allowed to land on Matinicus Rock, but they can circle it and you can get excellent views of most of the birds. In addition to the nesting species you might also see great and double-crested cormorants as well as common murres. If that wasn't enough you have a very good chance of seeing Minke whales, harbor porpoise and gray seals. If you get this far, see if your boat operator will take you around Seal Island. That is the site of a successful and on-going effort to restore puffins along with Arctic and common terns. Additional efforts are underway to attract nesting razorbills.

Your travels by boat will be a real adventure. Be prepared for cold, wind, spray and large swells and a trip lasting several hours. Also be prepared for great memories that will last a lifetime.

For travel to Matinicus Island:

By air, contact Telford Aviation at Knox Regional Airport (207) 596-5557 in Owls Head. They offer daily air taxi service to Matinicus. The flight takes ten minutes. Pets are welcome in their carriers. Call ahead for reservations and current prices.

By commercial boat, contact Offshore Freight and Passenger Service, Capt. Richard Moody, Matinicus, ME 04851 (207) 366-3700

By the Maine State Ferry Service call (207) 596-2202. Ferries run about once a month with vehicles and heavy freight.

For travel to Matinicus Rock contact:

Atlantic Expeditions, HC 35 Box 290, St. George, ME 04857 (207) 372-8621. Regular trips from Rockland.

Hardy Boat Cruises, PO Box 326, New Harbor, ME 04554 (800) 278-3346. Occasional trips from New Harbor.

Capt. Richard Moody, Matinicus Island, ME (207) 366-3700 or Albert Bunker (207) 366-3737

Down East

• *The Great Wass Island Preserve*

Wass Island is a spectacular 1,540-acre tract preserved by The Nature Conservancy and located in the town of Beals. It is largely pristine and has many outstanding natural features. Rare plants abound, including beach head iris, marsh felwort, blinks and bird's eye primrose. Many other plants are Arctic in nature, reaching the southern limit of their ranges. Also worthy of note is a large stand of jack pine, an almost bonsai-like tree living on soil so thin that few other species can survive. The bogs are thousands of years old, originating from sphagnum moss left by the retreating glaciers about 12,000 years ago.

You can observe nesting ospreys as well as bald eagles feeding and roosting in the preserve. You may also see palm warblers, Lincoln sparrows, boreal chickadees and spruce grouse. Just offshore you can see common eiders, blue herons and a variety of shore birds. On the ledges off Cape Cove, harbor seals congregate in numbers, frequently basking in the sun.

From Route 1 take ME 187 to Jonesport. Cross the bridge over the Moosabec Reach to Beals. Go through Beals to Great Wass Island. Follow the road (partially dirt) to Black Duck Cove, approximately three miles from Beals. Marked parking is on the left.

• *Machias Seal Island*

Machias Seal Island is a low island, very exposed to the sea, about 15 acres in size and 10 miles from the mainland. It is part of the United States although it has a light maintained by Canada. The island is home to large numbers of puffins and Arctic terns. You can also see rare and endangered razorbill auks and common murres.

The island can be reached by means of a commercial, guided tour. A motorboat ride takes you to the island where you carefully disembark to walk pathways or utilize blinds.

The trip out from Jonesport takes two-to-three hours with a stay of three hours.

More Info: Captain Barna B. Norton or Captain John E. Norton, RR 1, Box 990 Jonesport, ME 04649-9704 (207) 497-5933

• *Quoddy Head State Park*

Quoddy Head State Park is located at the extreme eastern point of the United States. It is a wonderful place to see a wide variety of birds. Look for Swainson's thrush, spruce grouse, boreal chickadee, blackpoll warbler and yellow-bellied flycatcher. Also look and listen for a variety of warblers to include American redstart, northern parula, common yellowthroat, Wilson's warblers and olive-sided flycatcher. Many other types of birds abound and out on the ledges you might also spot a great cormorant or black-legged kittiwake. A bonus sighting would be a whale, dolphin or porpoise, which frequent the rich feeding grounds off Quoddy Head.

From Route 1 take ME 189 toward Lubec. Just before Lubec proper, turn right onto South Lubec Road, then left onto West Quoddy Head following the signs to the lighthouse and State Park.

M o o s e h e a d   L a k e   &   K a t a h d i n

• *The Golden Road — A Drive from Millinocket to Greenville via the Pittston Farm*
This is a splendid way to experience the Great North Woods, timber harvesting both past and present while watching for birds and other wildlife. Getting an early start from Millinocket will give you a good chance of sighting moose, beaver and a wide variety of birds. This dirt road is in excellent condition and does not require four-wheel drive. However, you should be aware that logging trucks have the right of way and exercise it at high speeds. During dry periods they kick up a great deal of dust so be cautious and give the trucks a wide berth. The best policy is to pull to the side and stop. This is an all-day trip allowing for frequent stops (be sure to park well off the road) to observe the wildlife, mountain views, forestlands, wetlands, rock outcroppings, etc. During your many stops along the route you may well see black-backed woodpecker, gray jay, raven, crossbills and boreal chickadee.

When you get to Ripogenus Dam you might want to stop for a hiking and birding side trip. Then, continue along north of Moosehead Lake until you reach Seboomook Lake. At the end of the lake take the left turn south down to Pittston Farm for lunch.

Pittston Farm is located where the north and south branches of the Penobscot River meet and is a step back in history. The Great Northern Paper Company purchased the entire township of Pittston Academy Grant, including Pittston Farm, in 1906. By 1914 the farm included two large houses to accommodate large numbers of loggers. There were also three barns to hold 124 horses, a frost-proof vegetable house, a cannery, a slaughter house, an office, a water tower, a blacksmith shop, a boat house, a powerhouse, a carriage house and a company storehouse. Pittston Farm remained more or less active right up to 1971 when the end of the log drives marked the end of its usefulness. In 1992 Ken and Sonja Twitchell purchased Pittston Farm. After 15 months of restoration they opened Pittston Farm Lodge. Pittston Farm is now home to an inn, restaurant, sporting camp and campground. Visitors are greeted with homemade patchwork quilts, all-you-can-eat meals and warm hospitality. After lunch head south along the Greenville Rd. to Rockwood where you can look out onto Moosehead Lake and spectacular Mt. Kineo. From there continue south on Rts. 6/15 to Greenville.

Warning: There are no services along The Golden Road. Be sure to have a full tank of gas when you begin. Also be sure to bring along food, water and warm clothes in the event of a breakdown.

In DeLorme's Maine Atlas & Gazetteer follow the page sequence 43, 51, 50, 49, 48, 40 to 41.

For additional reading related to Birding — In Exceptional Places we would like to recommend the following book.

- A Birder's Guide to Maine, Elizabeth C. Pierson, Jan Erik Pierson, and Peter D. Vickery, Down East Books, Camden, ME, 399 pages

Boats & Boating

The Schooner Mary Day, courtesy of Maine Windjammer Association

Maine's unparalleled coastline, island waters, lakes and inland waterways comprise a boater's paradise, whether the choice is motor or sail, small or large, workboats, fishing boats, sailboats, kayaks and canoes, whitewater rafts or the magnificent windjammers that ply our coastal waters.

As a rule, of course, you're on your own aboard a boat — away from the crowds, enjoying the unique quiet and peace that is found only out on the water. And in this great state, you can enjoy the solitude of unspoiled woods and mountains in the morning and, by afternoon, be aboard a sleek sailboat putting a rail into the ocean under a refreshing breeze.

And if boating is more than just recreation to you — but a true love (as with many Mainers) — you can even visit some of the planet's most skilled boatbuilders and appreciate why what they do so well is considered a remarkable art form.

Here's a quick guide to put you on the right tack.

Tall Ship Sailing Adventures

The Maine Windjammer Association offers spectacular three-day and six-day sailing adventures on their 13 sailing ships, combining seafaring excitement with the majestic beauty and serenity of the Maine coast. Varied ports of call include uninhabited islands. Three square meals (including all the lobster you can eat), up close and personal with seabirds, lighthouses, seals, porpoises and often even whales. Passengers are invited to participate in all aspects of sailing, including taking the wheel and navigating. Prices are about $110 per person per day, all meals included. These boats sail out of Rockland, Rockport and Camden.

The fleet includes the following vessels:
- American Eagle — 92-foot schooner registered as a National Historic Landmark
- Angelique — 95-foot ketch
- Grace Bailey — 80-foot schooner
- Heritage — a newer boat (launched in 1983) built in the tradition of 19th-century coasting schooners
- Isaac H. Evans — another National Historic Landmark vessel
- J. & E. Riggin — National Historic Landmark status granted in 1991
- Lewis R. French — 64-foot schooner celebrating her 130th summer in Maine waters
- Mary Day — 90-foot schooner
- Mercantile — 78-foot schooner built in 1916
- Nathaniel Bowditch — 82-foot schooner, won Bermuda race in 1923
- Stephen Taber — 68-foot schooner built in 1871
- Timberwind — 70-foot pilot schooner built in 1931
- Victory Chimes — 132-foot schooner; the last three-masted schooner on the East Coast

These boats gather at several special events during the summer. Because they tend to draw large crowds, however, the preferred way to participate is aboard ship.

The schedule is as follows:
- Schooner Days, early June (place determined by weather)
- Windjammer Days, late June, Boothbay Harbor
- Great Schooner Race, early July
- Rockland Schooner Days, mid-July, Rockland
- Camden Windjammer Weekend, late August, Camden Harbor
- WoodenBoat Sail-In, early September, Brooklin

These magnificent boats are available for day sailing, trips of several days, weeklong trips, charters, parties or group excursions or, if you prefer, you can hire them out all by yourself. Whatever your choice, you'll find them safe, well maintained, ably crewed and simply a great way to enjoy a unique and memorable Maine vacation.

Maine Windjammer Association, PO Box 1144, Blue Hill, ME 04614
1-800-807-WIND
www.sailmainecoast.com

Other Sailing Trips and Cruises

Greater Portland

• Eagle Island Tours offers a number of different Casco Bay boat trips out of Portland — the Eagle Island, seal-watching, Portland Head Light and sunset cruises — at reasonable rates (i.e., $9 for adults, $6 for children; the trip to Eagle Island, including a visit to Adm. Robert E. Peary's summer home, is $17.50/$10.50). The company uses motor vessels with a capacity of 49 persons. Private charters to restaurants and islands also available.
Long Wharf on the waterfront, Portland, ME
(207) 774-6498
74 Raydon Road, York ME 03909
email: CWGLNAV@aol.com

Western Mountains & Lakes

• The Songo River Queen not only sounds like a Mississippi River boat, but looks like one, as well, as her paddle wheel propels her 90-foot hull up the Songo River between Sebago Lake and Brandy Pond and across Long Lake, with the western Maine mountains providing the backdrop.
P.O. Box 1226, Naples, ME 04055
(207) 693-6861

Midcoast

• The 64-foot windjammer Eastwind sails to the outer islands and Seal Rock out of Boothbay Harbor. Ask owners Herb and Doris Smith about their book, "Sailing Three Oceans." Per-person rates are $22; reservations are encouraged.
Eastwind at Fisherman's Wharf, Boothbay Harbor, ME
(207) 633-6598

• The Sylvina W. Beal, an 84-foot herring boat built in 1911, sails daily out of Boothbay Harbor — mornings, afternoons and sunsets, at $22 per person. You can find her tied up at the Boothbay Harbor Marina/Pier One.
P.O. Box 28, Cherryfield, ME 04622
(207) 546-2927 (winter) or (207) 633-1109 (summer)
www.downeastwindjammer.com
email: decruise@midmaine.com

• Muscongus Bay Cruises in Bremen offers a variety of cruises aboard both power and sailing vessels, including charters and group excursions and well as sailing instruction. Bareboat or captained.
289 Keene Neck Road, Bremen, ME 04551
(207) 529-4474
www.midcoast.com/~cruises
email: cruises@midcoast.com

• The 67-foot schooner Wendameen sails daily out of Rockland, drops anchor off the islands in Penobscot Bay and returns the following morning. $170-fare includes dinner and breakfast the following morning. Charters also available.
PO Box 252, Rockland, ME 04841
(207) 594-1751
www.schooneryacht.com/sail

• For a close-up look at seabirds, loons, seals and porpoises, plus a quick education about coastal geology and maritime history, get aboard the Olad, which sails out of Camden. Islands, lighthouses and the nature of Penobscot Bay. $20 per person. Nature programs vary, so call ahead.
Downeast Windjammers Packet Company, P.O. Box 432, Camden, ME 04843
(207) 236-2323
www.sailingsojourns.com
email: nugent@mint.net

• Cruise on the schooner Appledore out of Camden Harbor — daily cruises, sunset cruises, theme cruises as well as charters (49 passengers, up to 20 on overnight sails). When she's not at sea (or in the Keys during the winter), you can find her tied up at Sharp's Wharf next to the Camden Town Landing.
Zero Lily Pond Drive, Camden, ME 04843
(207) 236-8553

• The 72-foot schooner Bonnie Lynn sails out of Islesboro and visits the waters of Nova Scotia as well as New England (she's in the Grenadines in winter). She accommodates 25 passengers comfortably. Charter rates vary between $1,500-$2,000 per day up to $10,000 per week. If it's real privacy asea you want, you can book the Bonnie Lynn for two people for $9,000 per week.
The Schooner Bonnie Lynn, Islesboro, ME
(401) 862-1115
www.bonnielynn.com
email: information@BonnieLynn.com

• The small sloop Goddess of the Sea sails out of Tenants Harbor to offshore islands like Vinalhaven, Isle au Haut, Brimstone and Monhegan for afternoon cruises or one-day, two-day or three-day sailing adventures. You share the boat with no one other than your party and the crew. Rates range from $50 per person for the afternoon sail, $100 for the all-day sail, $160 for the overnight adventure, $260 for the two-day getaway and $390 for the three-day Downeast sail.
The Sloop Goddess of the Sea, Tenants Harbor, ME
(207) 314-1684, 1-888-724-5010
www.goddesscruise.com
email: capfrank@goddesscruise.com

• The Friendship sloop Surprise sails thrice daily out of Tenants Harbor; $30 per person for morning and afternoon trips, $25 for the sunset sail. Information available at the East Wind Inn:
(207) 372-6366 (1-800-241-VIEW)
www.friendshipsloop.com

• The Hardy III sails out of New Harbor and cruises Muscongus Bay, and includes historical presentations about the islands and villages being passed en route. You'll almost surely get to watch the seals in the bay, and may even catch a glimpse of puffins on the rocks nearby as you pass lighthouses and islands on the way to Monhegan Island.
P.O. Box 326, New Harbor, ME 04554
(207) 278-3346 (1-800-2PUFFIN)
www.hardyboat.com
email: cruises@hardyboat.com

Down East

• The spectacular 151-foot schooner Margaret Todd, the only four-masted schooner to ply New England waters in over half a century, puts to sea at Bar Harbor daily. The company also offers deep-sea fishing, plus ferry service to Winter Harbor, "the gateway to the Schoodic Peninsula."
The Sloop Margaret Todd, Bar Harbor Inn Pier, Bar Harbor, ME
(207) 288-4585 (summer) or (207) 546-2927 (winter)
www.downeastwindjammer.com

Fishing Excursions

Southern Coastal

• The 40-foot Bunny Clark out of Ogunquit specializes in helping you catch cod, pollock, halibut, haddock, hake, cusk and wolfish, and the crew will help you gaff and land the big ones (35 record breakers have been landed aboard since 1984). Everything — tackle, bait, the works — is provided. $30 per person half day, $50 for full day. Reservations required. Marathon trips available March through November.
P.O. Box 837F, Ogunquit, ME 03907
(207) 646-2214

• Also sailing out of Ogunquit is the Ugly Anne, a 44-foot motor vessel. All tackle and bait included. You catch 'em, they'll fillet 'em for you.
P.O. Box 683, Ogunquit, ME 03907
(207) 646-7202

Greater Portland

• Capt. Ben Garfield will take you out of South Portland on his 23-foot Fish Nautique for cod, pollock, shark, stripers, bluefish and mackerel. Full day, half day or custom charters. Go Fish! Charters, P.O. Box 10541, Portland, ME 04104
(207) 799-1339 or (207) 232-1678 (cell)

• You can go out aboard the Devil's Den from DiMillo's Marina in Portland and pursue tuna, shark, bluefish, stripers and more under the guidance of Capt. Harry Adams.
P.O. Box 272, Scarborough, ME 04070
(207) 761-4466

Midcoast

• If you can't avoid Freeport, and want something to do while somebody else is shopping, try the Freeport Family Charter service. Fishing cruises, nature cruises, lobstering cruises or just cruises. From LL Bean, take Bow Street to South Freeport Road, turn right and follow the road to the four-way stop. Turn left and follow to the harbor and look for Brewer's Marina on your left.
(207) 729-5903 or (207) 798-9542.

• You can take a lobster-fishing trip or just an "ecotour" aboard the MV Lively Lady Too out of Camden (Bayview Landing). Captain Alan Philbrick will show you how to haul traps, and if you just want to learn, he'll show you four major habitats of coastal wildlife — birds, seals and more. $20 for adults, $5 for children (ask about family rates, too).
(207) 236-6672 or (207) 839-7933 (in winter)

Down East

• Four-hour deep-sea fishing trips are available from the Bar Harbor Inn pier aboard the 50-foot MV Seal. Bait and tackle provided, $35 for adults, $20 for children.
(207) 288-4585 or (207) 288-2373.

Fun on the Water

Kennebec & Moose River Valleys

• Whitewater rafting on the Kennebec. The upper gorge offers a roller coaster trip over Big Mama, the Three Sisters and Magic Falls. Considered among the best whitewater experiences.
New England Outdoor Center, P.O. Box 669, Millinocket, ME 04462
1-800-766-7238
www.neoc.com
email: info@neoc.com

• Whitewater rafting on the Kennebec and Dead rivers — one-, two- and three-day excursions. Whitewater kayaking, too.
North Country Rivers, P.O. Box 47, East Vassalboro, ME 04935
(207) 672-4814 (summer), (207) 873-7257 (winter) or 1-800-348-8871
www.ncrivers.com
email: raftmaine@ncrivers.com

Moosehead Lake & Katahdin

• Moosehead Lake and Baxter State Park by canoe and kayak. Other Maine woods adventures also available.
Katahdin Outfitters, P.O. Box 34, Millinocket, ME 04462
(207) 723-5700 or 1-800-TO-CANOE
www.katahdinoutfitters.com
email: katoutfitters@etel.net

Maritime/Marine Museums

Southern Coastal

• Kittery Historical and Naval Museum — Kittery
  Maritime pieces and memorabilia, a shipbuilding exhibit and ship models reflecting the area's long and rich relationship with the sea.
Route 1, Kittery, ME
(207) 439-3080

Greater Portland

• Portland Harbor Museum — South Portland
  Changing and permanent exhibits of maritime and local history featuring the Snow Squall, the last American clipper ship, and the Spring Point Ledge Light. Tours of Fort Preble also offered. New exhibit in 2002 is called "What Ship is This: 300 Years of Ships in Portland Harbor."
Fort Road, South Portland, ME 04106
(207) 799-6337
www.portlandharbormuseum.org
email: portharbmuseum@juno.com

Also worth checking into is the Maine Maritime Heritage Trail.
1-800-MAINE45

Midcoast

• Maine Watercraft Museum — Thomaston
  The third largest collection of small craft in the country, with primary emphasis on boats built in the state of Maine. This is a unique in-the-water hands-on museum.
4 Knox Street Landing, Thomaston, ME 04861
(207) 354-0444
www.midcoast.com/~oldboats
email: oldboats@midcoast.com

• Maine Maritime Museum — Bath
  Maine's colorful maritime history is presented through gallery exhibits, a shipyard site, special events and narrated excursions along the Kennebec River and the coast to points of historic significance. The shipyard, where more than 40 four-, five- and six-masted schooners were built between 1894 and 1920, is faithfully

preserved, tools and all. You can board and even cruise on the Sherman Zwicker, a Grand Banks fishing schooner. The exhibits of the museum are well done and ever changing. And if you wish, you can get there by boat via their docks on the Kennebec River, just a short distance downstream from the Bath Iron Works.
243 Washington Street, Bath, ME 04530
(207) 443-1316
www.bathmaine.com
email: Maritime@bathmaine.com

• Penobscot Marine Museum — Searsport
    Dedicated to preserving and presenting Maine's rich maritime heritage. 13 historic buildings with galleries, exhibits, collections, archives, library and activities.
5 Church Street, PO Box 498, Searsport, ME 04974
(207) 548-2529
www.penobscotmarinemuseum.org
email: museumoffices@penobscotmarinemuseum.org

Moosehead Lake & Katahdin

• Moosehead Marine Museum — Greenville
    Exhibits focus on logging, the lumberman and the Maine Guide. If you get the chance to talk with the genial Executive Director, Duke McKeil, he'll give you some great insights into this remote part of our world. Point of departure for the SS Katahdin, the 225-seat tour boat (originally a towboat for moving logs across the lake), which offers cruises on Moosehead Lake, including around Mt. Kineo. This boat is also available for charter, weddings and parties.
P.O. Box 1151, Greenville, ME 04441
(207) 695-2716
www.katahdincruises.com

Boatbuilders

• Hinckley Yachts — Southwest Harbor
    One of the world's premier builders of custom and semi-custom yachts, both motor and sail.
(207) 244-5531
www.thehinckleyco.com

• Morris Yachts — Bass Harbor
   Designers and builders of world-class sailing yachts.
(207) 244-5509
www.morrisyachts.com
email: sales@morrisyachts.com

• Lyman Morse Boatbuilding — Thomaston
   If you have a plan, or just a general idea, of the boat you want, these folks can build it for you just the way you want it.
www.lymanmorse.com
email: cabot@lymanmorse.com

• Sabre Yachts — Raymond
   A leading producer of motor and sailing yachts.
(207) 655-3831
www.sabreyachts.com
email: sabre@sabreyachts.com

   Maine also boasts over 100 private boatbuilders, each quite worthy of a visit — but not generally open to public tours. They range from the prize-winning wooden boat builder Ralph Stanley of Southwest Harbor to the internationally-renown Tim Hodgdon of Boothbay Harbor, builder of the recently-launched 124-foot sloop Antonisa. Who knows — a polite call well in advance might just earn you a tour.
   See you aboard!

Camping & Real Camps

Courtesy of King & Bartlett Fish & Game Club

Camps and campgrounds can be found throughout Maine, and right from the southern border they line the primary tourist arteries. Our idea of a camp, however, is not RVs or trailers parked cheek-to-jowl, and it's probably not yours, either.

The camps listed here are very special and often very remote. We believe that "camp" means something removed from ordinary life, and should offer a unique Maine experience. These camps fit that bill. For the most part, they are members of the Maine Sporting Camp Association, and as such abide by a code of ethics that promotes and protects the tradition of Maine sporting camping and the preservation of natural resources. It also assures responsible attitudes and safe outdoor activities by all who are involved in the great outdoors.

Most of these camps offer American plan accommodations, which means three hearty meals; some offer housekeeping, as well. Although it varies from camp to camp, you can expect to enjoy boating, biking, canoeing and kayaking, bird-watching, moose-watching and hiking, hunting and fishing as well as cross-country skiing, snowmobiling and other winter activities. MSCA members will also recommend other camps that offer activities they may be unable to provide.

If you want the real Maine camp experience, or want to pitch your tent in a special place, this is where to look.

Western Mountains & Lakes

Dead River/Flagstaff Lake Area

• King & Bartlett Fish & Game Club
PO Box 4, Eustis, ME 04936
(207) 243-2956
www.kingandbartlett.com

• Tim Pond Camps
PO Box 22, Eustis, ME 04936
(207) 243-2947
www.timpondcamps.com
email: info@timpondcamps.com

Ellis River/Ellis Pond Area

• Lakewood Camps
PO Box 282, Andover, ME 04216
(207) 243-2959
www.lakewoodcamps.com

Rangeley Lake Area

• Bosebuck Mountain Camps
PO Box 1213, Rangeley, ME 04970
(207) 446-2825
www.bosebuck.com

• Grant's Kennebago Camps
PO Box 786, Rangeley, ME 04970
1-800-633-4815
www.grantcamps.com
email: grants@rangeley.org

Down East

Grand Lake/Big Lake Area

• Indian Rock Camps
PO Box 117, Grand Lake Stream, ME 04637

(207) 796-2822, 1-800-498-2821
www.nemaine.com/indianrock/index.htm
email: indianrockcamp@nemaine.com

• Canal Side Cabins
PO Box 77, Canal St., Grand Lake Stream, ME 04637
(207) 796-2796
www.canalsidecabins.com
email: info@canalsidecabins.com

• The Pines Lodge
PO Box 158, Grand Lake Stream, ME 04637
(207) 557-7463
www.thepineslodge.com
email: info@thepineslodge.com

• Weatherby's, The Fisherman's Resort
PO Box 69, Grand Lake Stream, ME 04637
(207) 796-5558
www.weatherbys.com
email: weather@somtel.com

• Leen's Lodge
PO Box 40, Grand Lake Stream, ME 04637
1-800-99-LEENS
www.leenslodge.com

Dennys River Dennys Bay Area

• Robinson's Cottages
Rt. 86, Dennysville, ME 04628
(207) 726-3901
www.robinsonscottages.com
email: robinson@midmaine.com

Kennebec & Moose River Valleys

Messalonskee Lake area

• Alden Camps
Alden Camps Road, Oakland, ME 04963

(207) 465-7703
www.aldencamps.com
email: alden@mint.net

Wood Pond/Attean Pond Area

• Hardscrabble Lodge
PO Box 459, Jackman, ME 04945
(207) 243-3020
www.hardscrabble.org

• The Last Resort
PO Box 777, Jackman, ME 04945
(207) 668-5091, 1-800-441-5091
www.themainelink.com/lastresort
email: lastres@moosehead.net

• Bulldog Camps
HC64, Box 554, Jackman, ME 04945
(207) 243-2853
www.bulldogcamps.com

• Cedar Ridge Outfitters
PO Box 744, Attean Road, Jackman, ME 04945
(207) 668-4169
www.cedarridgeoutfitters.com
email: info@cedarridgeoutfitters.com

Moosehead Lake & Katahdin

Moosehead Lake Area

• Gentle Ben's Lodge
PO Box 212, Rockwood, ME 04478
(207) 534-2201, 1-800-242-3769
www.gentleben.com
email: info@gentleben.com

• Brassau Lake Camps
PO Box 187, Rockwood, ME 04478

(207) 534-7328
www.connectmaine.com/brassau

• The Birches Resort
    Wilderness expeditions and tours.
PO Box 41, Rockwood ME 04478
(207) 534-7305
www.birches.com
email: wwld@aol.com

• Frost Pond Camps
HCR 76, Box 620, Greenville, ME 04441
(207) 695-2821
www.frostpondcamps.com
email: frostpond@gwi.net

• Nugent-McNally's Camps
HCR 76, Box 632, Greenville, ME 04441
(207) 944-5991
www.nugent-mcnallycamps.com
email: regina@acadia.net

• Little Lyford Pond Camps
PO Box 340, Greenville, ME 04441
(207) 280-0016
www.littlelyford.com
email: info@littlelyford.com

• Medawisla Wilderness Camps
HCR 76, Box 592, Greenville, ME 04441
(207) 695-2690
www.medawisla.com

Mattanawcook Pond Area

• Eagle Lodge & Camps
PO Box 686, Lincoln, ME 04457
(207) 794-2181
www.eaglelodgemaine.com
email: eaglodge@aol.com

Millinocket/Ferguson Lake Area

• Katahdin Lake Wilderness Camp
PO Box 398, Millinocket, ME 04462
(207) 723-4050
www.katahdinlakecamps.com
email: t3r8lake@ime.net

• Nahmakanta Lake Camps
PO Box 544, Millinocket, ME 04462
(207) 746-7356
www.nahmakanta.com
email: info@nahmakanta.com

• Buckhorn Camps
PO Box 639, Millinocket, ME 04462
(207) 745-5023
www.mainesnowmobile.com/buckhorn.html
email: buckhorn@kai.net

Patten/Thousand Acre Bog Area

• Bowlin Camps
PO Box 251, Patten, ME 04765
(207) 528-2022
www.bowlincamps.com

• Macannamac Camps
PO Box 696, Patten, ME 04765
(207) 528-2855
www.macannamac.com

South Branch Lake Area

• South Branch Lake Camps
HCR 66, Lake Road, Box 195, Seboeis, ME 04448
(207) 732-3446, 1-800-248-0554
www.southbranchlakecamps.com
email: sobranch@midmaine.com

Far North

Mattawamkeag Lake Area

• Bear Mountain Lodge
RR #1 Box 1969, Smyrna Mills, ME 04780
(207) 528-2124
www.mainerec.com/bearmt.html

Musquash/Farrow Lake Area

• The Birches Cabins
603 Lakeview Road, Topsfield, ME 04490
(207) 796-5517
www.thebirchescabins.com
email: birchescabins@microgate.net

Machias/Aroostook River Area

• Libby Camps
PO Box 810, Ashland, ME 04732
(207) 435-8274
www.libbycamps.com
email: matt@libbycamps.com

• Bradford Camps
PO Box 729, Ashland, ME 04732
(207) 746-7777
www.bradfordcamps.com
email: maine@bradfordcamps.com

Grand Lake/Crooked Brook Area

• Rideouts Lakeside Lodge & Cottages
RR #1 Box 64, Danforth, ME 04424
(207) 448-2440, 1-800-594-5391
www.rideouts.com
email: info@rideouts.com

Bangor/Penobscot River Area

• Great Pond Wilderness Lodge & Sporting Camps
672 Main Road, Eddington, ME 04428
(207) 745-6728

Oxbow/Aroostook River Area

• Homestead Lodge
Oxbow Road, Oxbow, ME 04764
(207) 435-6357
www.homesteadlodgemaine.com

• Umcolcus Sporting Camps
1243 Oxbow Road, Oxbow, ME 04764
(207) 897-4056
www.umcolcus.com
email: umcolcus@mfx.net

Big Lake/Lewy Lake Area

• Long Lake Camps
PO Box 817, Princeton, ME 04668
(207) 796-2051
www.longlakecamps.com
email: longlake@nemaine.com

Portage Lake Area

• Moose Point Camps
PO Box 170, Portage, ME 04768
(207) 435-6156
www.moosepoitcamps.com

• Crooked Tree Lodge & Camps
PO Box 203, Portage, ME 04768
(207) 435-6413
www.crookedtreelodgemaine.com
email: info@crookedtreelodge.com

• Red River Camps
PO Box 320, Portage, ME 04768

(207) 43506000
www.redrivercamps.com
email: rbrophy@ainop.com

Baskaheegan Lake Area

• Wheaton's Lodge & Camps
  Fisherman's paradise (two world-record smallmouth in last nine seasons).
HC 81 Box 120, Brookton, ME 04413
(207) 448-7723
www.wheatonslodge.com
email: wheatons1@hotmail.com

Presque Isle Area

• Willard Jalbert Camps
6 Winchester Street, Presque Isle, ME 04769
(207) 764-0494
email: riverat@interport.com

Camping in Maine State Parks

Several Maine State Parks offer superb camping in a variety of settings. Most campsites offer facilities up to and including hot showers. Here are the favorites.

Western Mountains & Lakes

• Sebago Lake State Park — Casco
  A forested lakeside park with 1,400 acres of foothills, ponds, bogs, a river and, of course, the sandy beaches (and fishing) on Maine's second largest lake.
Route 1 between Naples and South Casco.
(207) 693-6613
Sebago Lake State Park, 11 Park Access Road, Casco, ME 04055

• Mt. Blue State Park — Weld
  Spectacular mountain views from this lakeside park, with a network of trails, a boat launch and a thousand perfect places for a picnic to be shared with moose, coyote and, perhaps, even a black bear.
Take Rt. 156 northwest from Wilton for 14 miles.
(207) 585-2347
Mt. Blue State Park, RR #1, Box 610, Weld, ME 04285

• Rangeley Lake State Park — Rangeley
    This incomparable mountain campsite offers everything — especially if you like to fish for your breakfast. Great wintertime snowmobiling, too.
Rt. 17 from Rumford or Rt. 4 from Farmington.
(207) 864-3858
Rangeley Lake State Park, HC 32, Box 5000, Rangeley, ME 04970

M i d c o a s t

• Bradbury Mountain State Park — Pownal
    Easily accessed, between Portland and Lewiston-Auburn, Bradbury Mountain offers wonderful views from its summit, and lots of hiking trails, camp sites, snowshoe trails and more.
Near Pownal, five miles from the Freeport-Durham exit on I-95.
(207) 688-4712
Bradbury Mountain State Park, 528 Hallowell Road, Pownal, ME 04069

• Camden Hills State Park — Camden
    There may be no vista in all of New England more magnificent than the one from atop Mt. Battie in Camden Hills State Park. Penobscot Bay lies before you in panorama, and on a clear day, you can even see Cadillac Mountain in Acadia National Park.
Two miles north of Camden on Route 1.
(207) 236-3109
Camden Hills State Park, 280 Belfast Road, Camden, ME 04843

• Warren Island State Park — Lincolnville
    This park is located on an island in Penobscot Bay, and can only be reached by boat. Once there, you're in for a unique experience.
(207) 236-3109
Warren Island State Park, P.O. Box 105, Lincolnville, ME 04849

M o o s e h e a d   L a k e   &   K a t a h d i n

• Lily Bay State Park — Moosehead Lake
    This 920-acre park is on Beaver Cove, on the eastern shore of Moosehead Lake, at 117 square miles, Maine's largest lake. Rising majestically from its middle is the spectacular Mt. Kineo, an 800-foot rock that beckons climbers. Troll for togue, brook trout and landlocked salmon en route.
Nine miles north of Greenville.

(207) 695-2700
Lily Bay State Park, HC 76, Box 425, Greenville, ME 04441

Far North

• Aroostook State Park — Presque Isle
    Maine's first state park is an ideal jumping off place for exploring the North Woods, the Allagash and the provinces of Quebec and New Brunswick — the way the first explorers did.
Echo Lake, off Route 1 south of Presque Isle
(207) 768-8341
Aroostook State Park, 87 State Park Road, Presque Isle, ME 04769

• Allagash Wilderness Waterway
    If it's camping by canoe you desire, this is paradise — a 92-mile corridor of lakes and rivers through the vast North Woods. Good snowmobiling (albeit no groomed trails) in winter, as well as good ice fishing.
(207) 941-4014
Allagash Wilderness Waterway, c/o Bureau of Parks & Lands, 106 Hogan Road, Bangor, ME 04401

Note: For more information on these and other state parks, as well as public lands, go to www.state.me.us and click on "Reserve a campsite."

Historic Chapels & Churches

St. Peter's-by-the-Sea Chapel, Cape Neddick, by Kathryn Gile Carter

The earliest houses of worship in Maine, as in other parts of New England, were the meeting houses. They tended to dominate their towns and villages and were the center of community life. The early Yankees met here for all honorable purposes, both sacred and secular and hence the name, meeting house. It was an edifice ideally suited to the Puritan ethic of "a church without a bishop and a state without a king." The meeting house was secular looking, often without a tower or ornamentation and with the entry door along the wider side of the building, not unlike a house.

Soon after the Revolution, the ties between church and state were broken and meeting houses tended to become either secular buildings or, through architectural innovation, identifiable houses of worship. Massachusetts architects like Charles Bulfinch and Asher Benjamin created the classic style church we so readily identify with today in Maine and the rest of New England. The church door was set in a wide bay on the narrow, gabled end, often flanked by two smaller doors. A tower was added that sat atop the bay. The roofs were much less steeply pitched and ornamentation such as Palladian windows and pilasters were added. Most of the meeting houses that evolved into classic churches housed members of the Congregational denomination. Over time, Episcopalians, Baptists, Methodists, Universalists, Quakers and Roman Catholics realized equality under law and created their own houses of worship.

In the late 1800s, Maine became a fashionable summer destination and many wealthy families from Philadelphia, New York and Boston spent their entire summers in small enclaves along the Maine coast. They wished to continue worshiping in their own denomination and so, mostly between 1890 and 1910, built a chain of 18 exquisitely crafted chapels from York to Sorrento.

For many visitors, attending service at a summer chapel or historic church is an important part of the Maine experience. It's a way of extending your regular religious practice, but in a setting consistent with your desire for change and renewal. The old churches and chapels of Maine are wonderful places to restore your soul. But if you're just visiting them for their architectural and historic value, you'll also find yourself blessed.

S o u t h e r n   C o a s t a l

• First Congregational Church (1730)
Rt. 103, Kittery, Maine
The first church organized in Maine was in York, the second at Wells and the third at Kittery. However, this building is the oldest standing church in Maine. It is very plain and simple with one door in front and two windows to either side. The original door on the long side was closed in 1840 and the entrance moved to the narrow, gabled side. The church was also turned to face the new road in 1874. Sir William Pepperell, conqueror of the French stronghold Louisburg in 1745, worshiped here . His mansion, the 1760 Lady Pepperell House, is very nearby. The grave of poet Celia Thaxter is in the adjacent graveyard.

• St. Martin's in the Field — Episcopal Summer Chapel
St. Martin's Lane, Biddeford Pool, ME 04006

• St. Peter's-by-the-Sea — Episcopal Summer Chapel
Shore Road (near Cliff House), Cape Neddick, ME 03902
The cornerstone for this beautiful stone church in the Romanesque style was laid in 1897. Summer services have been held continuously ever since. It is a favorite location for many Southern Coastal weddings.

• First Parish Church (1773)
Kennebunk, ME
The people of Kennebunk were originally required by law to attend church in Wells. For seven years they petitioned for a separate parish, but were refused in the Wells town meetings. Finally they won an appeal of their case in the General Court of Massachusetts (Maine then being part of that state). They then formed the Second Congregational Society in 1750 and located their church at

Kennebunk Landing until 1773. In that year they moved the congregation to Kennebunk Village where they built a meeting house, the present church. In 1803 village growth necessitated a larger church and, instead of building a new one, they found a different solution. They simply cut the current church in two, moved the rear portion back 28 feet, and built walls joining the two halves. A tower and steeple were completed in 1804 and a bell installed. The bell was cast in the foundry of Paul Revere & Sons of Boston.

• St. Philip's by the Sea — Episcopal Summer Chapel
3 Neptune Lane, Fortunes Rock, Biddeford, ME 04005

• Trinity Chapel — Episcopal Summer Chapel
Woodland Avenue, Kennebunk Beach, ME 04043
   Trinity was formerly a private chapel, unused for 25 years. The chapel was restored after much neglect and services have continued since 1949. The chapel houses an impressive collection of ship's models.

• St. Ann's — Episcopal Summer Chapel
Ocean Avenue, Kennebunkport, ME 04046

• St. James' Chapel — Episcopal Summer Chapel
Prouts Neck, ME 04074
   This chapel was built in 1885, consecrated in 1890 and dedicated to the patron saint of fishermen. The younger brother of the painter Winslow Homer founded it.

• Trinity Chapel — Episcopal Summer Chapel
914 York Street, York Harbor, ME 03911
   This beautiful stone edifice had its origins back in 1884 with a small wooden church. The cornerstone for the current chapel was laid in 1908 with the first service in 1910. The chapel houses a beautiful Tiffany stained-glass window over the altar.

Greater Portland

• Cathedral of the Immaculate Conception — Roman Catholic
307 Congress Street, Portland, ME 04101-3638
(207) 773-7746
   This cathedral was built immediately after the Civil War and, by design, was the largest cathedral in America at that time. Construction of the brick and slate roof edifice took place from 1866 to 1869. This Neogothic style cathedral was placed on the National Register of Historic Places on June 20, 1985.

Midcoast

• All Saints by the Sea — Episcopal Summer Chapel
Washington Avenue, Bailey Island, ME 04003
   Civil War hero, Governor of Maine and President of Bowdoin College Joshua Chamberlain took a steamer from Portland to attend the first service of what would become All Saints by the Sea.

• All Saints Chapel — Episcopal Summer Chapel
Orr's Island, ME 04006
   Community services have been practiced here since 1892 and the current chapel was consecrated in 1900. Bailey and Orr's are adjoining islands. The Labor Day service is held at All Saints, Orr's Island, on even numbered years and at All Saints by the Sea, Bailey Island, on odd numbered years.

• Old Meeting House (1757)
Harpswell Center, ME
   Congregationalists built this classic meeting house in 1757 when they established themselves as a parish apart from the Town of Yarmouth. The building has been kept in its original condition, even though for many years it was used as the town hall. The Old Meeting House interior was exceptionally simple. Handmade boards and clapboards were made extra thick to keep out the cold. In the Deacon's box, there is one floorboard over 29 inches wide. This apparently was an effort to flout the King's law that all trees over 24 inches in diameter be reserved for masts for the British Navy. Harpswell's Meeting House is now a National Historic Monument.

• Nequasset Meeting House (1757)
Woolwich, ME
   This meeting house sits on the east bank of the Kennebec River, across from Bath. It is the oldest meeting house east of the Kennebec, having been built in 1757. Josiah Winship was the first pastor, ordained by Congregationalists in 1765.

• Vesper Hill Chapel (The Children's Chapel) — Non-denominational Summer Chapel
Chapel Lane, Rockport, ME 04856
   This open-sided and extraordinary chapel is dedicated to the memory of all children who have been lost to their families. It is set in a beautiful garden with a magnificent view out to sea. Getting there is a bit tricky. From the center of Rockport, go up the hill to the small traffic island, turn right onto Russell Avenue. Go about a quarter to a half mile and take a right onto Calderwood Lane (if you see the Belted Galloways Farm sign, you've gone too far). Continue on Calderwood through golf club fairways on both sides to top of hill. At top of hill

turn right onto dirt lane (Chapel Lane). The Chapel is on your immediate left.
For more info: Vesper Hill Foundation, Lynn Johnson, (207) 236-0603

• St. Patrick's — Roman Catholic Church
On the old road from Newcastle to Damariscotta Mills, Newcastle, ME 04553

This is the oldest Catholic church both in Maine and New England. It was begun in 1807 and completed in 1808. The church was designed for endurance with the walls made one-and-one-half-foot thick. The small odd-shaped bricks with which the church was built were made across Damariscotta Lake and hauled by oxen across the ice in the Winter of 1807. The church was built primarily through the largess of Matthew Cottrill and James Kavanagh, Irish immigrants and prosperous partners in trade in Damariscotta Mills. They were encouraged in their endeavor by Father (later Bishop) John Cheverus of Boston, who dedicated the church on July 17, 1808.

• Christ Church — Episcopal Summer Chapel
Dark Harbor, Islesboro, ME 04848

This island chapel has been in existence since 1892.

• Our Lady of the Evergreens — Episcopal Summer Chapel
PO Box 94, Harborside, ME 04642

• German Meeting House (c. 1770)
Waldoboro, ME

The German Lutherans who arrived in 1748 named their settlement for General Samuel Waldo, proprietor of the Waldo Patent that spanned thousands of acres. The proprietor had apparently provided the prospective settlers with reason to believe they would receive more than they did. In the graveyard, one of the stones is inscribed, "This town was settled in 1748 by Germans who migrated to this place with the promise and expectation of finding a prosperous city, instead of which they found nothing but a wilderness." These Lutherans met regularly for Sabbath services without a minister for 20 years. The present meeting house was built about 1770 on the east bank of the Medomak River.

• St. Cuthbert's Chapel — Episcopal Summer Chapel
MacMahan Island, ME 04046

At the time of its organization in 1894, this summer chapel was the only congregation in the world named after St. Cuthbert

• Walpole Meeting House (1772)
South Bristol, ME

The original name for Bristol was Walpole, but in 1767 the name was changed to Bristol, reflecting the fact that many of the inhabitants had come from Bristol, England. However, the meeting house retained the Walpole name when it was built in 1772. There were also many Scots in the area and the church was organized as Presbyterian. The first pastor was the Reverend Alexander McLain, a Scottish Presbyterian. From the outside, the meeting house looks very much like a house, but inside it was designed as a church in the style of the period.

• All Saints by the Sea — Episcopal Summer Chapel
Southport Island, ME 04569
This unusual chapel was built in 1905 and consecrated in 1906. Its services may be reached by boat, as it may be Maine's only chapel with its own dock and float. Private boats are welcome to dock for services.

• St. George's Chapel — Episcopal Summer Chapel
Tenants Harbor, ME 04869
This straightforward wooden building in a rustic setting has been in existence since 1901. It may best be described today as it was in 1902, "small and simple yet wholly adequate."

• Alna Meeting House (1789)
Alna, ME
This meeting house was very well built with hand-hewn 12-by-14-inch beams. With the exception of the wide entry bay, it looks very much like a residence. The exterior design is two-story, plain rectangular with no ornamentation. Inside, the church's high pulpit accommodated preachers of various heights in a novel way. Sliding shelves at varying heights allowed each preacher to select his most comfortable position to address the congregation. The first preacher was Jonathan Scott who officiated prior to organization. The Congregational Society was formally organized in 1796 and the Revered Jonathan Ward assumed duties as pastor until 1818.

Down East

• Church of the Redeemer — Episcopal Summer Chapel
Sorrento, ME 04677

• St. Christopher by the Sea — Episcopal Summer Chapel
Grindstone Neck, Winter Harbor, ME 04693
Services have been held here since 1893. The chapel houses a wooden panel of Christ and two disciples carved circa 1509-11.

Covered Bridges
(and other unusual crossings)

Lovejoy Bridge, Andover, by John Brough

There is something quite special about bridges, particularly old bridges. Perhaps they make us feel connected — connected not only in a geographic sense, but connected in time. They are among the most beautiful of Maine's many landmarks yet are rarely visited. They cross salt water with strong tidal flows as well as powerful rivers and meandering streams. Many are wooden covered bridges, some are built on pilings or great slabs of rock and several are suspension bridges made of steel. They are all quite unique, all quite charming. To find most of them, you have to get off the beaten path. They are often set in wonderfully bucolic sites that are perfect for a picnic.

Here are several that will help make your visit to The Pine Tree State truly memorable.

Southern Coastal

• Babb's Bridge

Babb's Bridge was built in 1864, but burned in 1973. The current bridge is an exact replica, built in 1973 and opened to traffic in 1976. It is located 2.5 miles north of South Windham, then half a mile west, over the Presumpscot River between the towns of Gorham and Windham.

• Grist Mill Bridge

This is a stone and timber structure that spans the Little River and is located about three miles south of East Lebanon on the Little River Road. It is composed of laid rubblestone, rising about 13 feet above the river. It is 54 feet long and 24 feet wide. Its current design dates from the early 1950s when it replaced a structure utilizing round logs for stringers, a plank deck and guardrails of triangular supports linked by a wooden rail. In 1993 a major renovation project replaced the timber superstructure in kind and restored the stone pier and abutments. The bridge was entered into the National Register of Historic Places in 1990.

• Sewall's Bridge

This bridge over the York River was built in 1761 on wood pilings, and was the first piling-design drawbridge built in America. The pilings were of varying lengths, driven into the river bottom by dropping heavy oak logs on them. The original bridge was so well built that it remained in use until 1934, when it was replaced with a similarly designed woodpile bridge. The bridge is in regular use today and was dedicated as a historic civil engineering landmark in 1986. You can park nearby at the Hancock Wharf, once owned by the very same John Hancock who signed the Declaration of Independence. At the same location you might take in an art exhibit at the small, but highly regarded Marshall Store Gallery.

Western Mountains & Lakes

• Artist's Covered Bridge

Built in 1872, this bridge is called the Artist's Bridge because it has been so often photographed and painted. This 87-foot Paddleford truss bridge has been closed to traffic since 1958. It spans the Sunday River about four miles northwest of North Bethel in Newry. If you have a photographic or artistic bent you might well make you own attempt to capture the essence of this very special bridge. So be sure to pack your camera or canvas as well as a picnic lunch.

• Bennett Bridge

This 93-foot Paddleford truss bridge was built in 1901. It was closed to traffic in 1985. It spans the Magalloway River and is located 1.5 miles south of Wilson Mills. If you really want to get away from it all, this is the bridge for you. You are close to New Hampshire and definitely "in the country."

• Hemlock Bridge

This beauty was built in 1857 and has a Paddleford truss span of 109 feet. The bridge was reinforced to carry traffic in 1988. It is located three miles northwest of East Fryeburg, over an old channel of the Saco River. This is your "classic" covered bridge.

• Lovejoy Bridge

This Paddleford truss bridge spanning only 70 feet was built in 1868 and is the shortest of Maine's covered bridges. It was reinforced in 1984 to carry local traffic. It is located in South Andover and spans the Ellis River. It is "short," but "sweet," so you would do well to spend some time walking and viewing it from several vantage points.

• Parsonfield-Porter Bridge

The towns of Porter and Parsonfield collaborated to build this bridge in 1859. It is a 152-foot Paddleford construction, strengthened with laminated wood arches. The bridge was closed to traffic in 1960. It is located half a mile south of Porter and spans the Ossipee River.

Midcoast

• Bailey Island Bridge

This bridge connects Bailey Island with Orr's Island. The bridge design presented unique problems because of the strong tidal flows separating the islands. Construction was authorized in 1926 and an unusual crib bridge design was used. The bridge incorporates granite slabs sufficiently heavy to withstand the pressures of winds and tides. The slabs were then surrounded by open wood cribbing that permitted the free ebb and flow of tidal currents. A concrete road was built on top of the granite cribs. In 1951 a sidewalk was added to the bridge, followed by guardrails in 1961. In 1984 the Bailey Island Bridge was dedicated as an historic civil engineering landmark. It is listed on the National Register of Historic Places.

Kennebec & Moose River Valleys

• New Portland Wire Bridge

This unique wire suspension bridge spans 198 feet over the Carrabassett River. It is the only survivor of four such bridges built in Maine in the 1800s, and may be the only such bridge still standing in the country. Construction began in 1864 and was completed in 1866. The towers are constructed of timber framing and covered with boards protected by cedar shingles. In 1959 Maine enacted legislation for the preservation of the bridge. It was renovated in 1961 when the tower bases were capped with concrete, the towers were rebuilt, steel suspender rods were replaced by steel cables, and a new timber deck installed. The tower framing timbers and main support cables are original.

• Ticonic Two Cent Bridge

This is a long, "must walk across," pedestrian suspension bridge over the Kennebec River. Park in the lot along the river in downtown Waterville, then walk across to Winslow. You can follow the footsteps of the mill workers who made their way between the two towns in the early 1900s, paying two cents for the crossing. The Berlin Construction Company of Connecticut built the bridge in 1901-2 at a cost of $6,500. When you get across to Winslow, climb the low hill in the gardens for a nice look back at Waterville.

Moosehead Lake & Katahdin

• Lowes Bridge

The flood of April 1, 1987, washed away the original bridge built in 1857. A more modern bridge, patterned after the original, was built on the original abutments in 1990. It spans 120 feet over the Piscataquis River. It is located just off ME15 south of Guilford Village.

• Robyville Bridge

This bridge, built in 1876, is the only completely-shingled covered bridge in Maine. It spans 73 feet and is of Long truss design. It was reinforced in 1984 to carry local traffic. It crosses Kenduskeag Stream in Robyville Village in the town of Corinth about three miles northwest of Kenduskeag Village.

Far North

• Watson Settlement Bridge

This bridge, built in 1911, is the northernmost and youngest of Maine's covered bridges. It has timber trusses of the Howe design and has two spans totaling 170 feet. In 1984 the bridge was closed to local traffic. It spans Meduxnekeag Stream and is located in the town of Littleton on the Littleton-to-Woodstock road.

Select Dining

Courtesy of The White Barn Inn, Kennebunk Beach

You'll want to be sure to get your fill of lobster while in Maine, of course, (and you'll have no trouble finding places that offer them), but finding other places for an enjoyable dining experience without being crushed — or having to wait in line — is a bit more challenging.

The following carefully-culled list of restaurants will help you find those "secret" places, dining gems that offer something special. And you'll find many of the favorites where the locals like to go, as yet not overrun with tourists.

They range from semi-formal (in essence, formal dining seems to have been banned in Maine) to casual and even very casual; clambakes to French cuisine and everything in between. Prices cover the entire spectrum.

Most are off the busy trail, but close enough to it that you can readily access the places you'll want to see and enjoy to make your visit to Maine a truly memorable experience.

Bon appetit!

Southern Coastal

• Chauncey Creek — Kittery Point
A traditionally fun way to enjoy Maine lobster — outdoors, on the creek. Bring your own fixin's and drinks. (207) 439-1030

• Harbor Porches at Stage Neck Inn — York Harbor
Fine dining in a beautiful room with nothing but glass between you and panoramic views of the ocean. Varied menu. Moderate-to-expensive. (207) 363-3850

• Dockside Restaurant — York Harbor
Called one of the best dockside restaurants on the coast by Down East magazine. "Dublin Lawyer Lobster," knockout chowder and other outstanding dishes served on an island overlooking the harbor and the York River. Moderate-to-expensive. (207) 363-2722

• Clay Hill Farm — Ogunquit
A back-country farmhouse in a beautiful wooded setting with excellent food. Moderate-to-expensive. (207) 361-2272

• White Barn Inn — Kennebunk Beach
A top-rated restaurant, almost-formal dining with super service. Expensive. (207) 967-2321

• Cape Arundel Inn — Kennebunkport
Fast becoming one of the area's favorites. Fine dining with spectacular ocean views. Moderate-to-expensive. (207) 967-2125

• The Nonantum Resort — Kennebunkport
Native Maine seafood as well as traditional European and American favorites overlooking the Kennebunk River. Moderate-to-expensive. (207) 967-4050

• The Lobster Pot — Cape Porpoise
Everything from steak to burgers, but lobster is the big attraction. (207) 967-4607

• Lobster Claw — Saco
Lobsters cooked in huge pots outside, served up with chowder, steamers and/or fried seafood inside. Take out, too. (207) 282-0040

Greater Portland

• Fore Street — Portland
Gourmet cuisine, artfully served in a huge old warehouse (converted to provide a very pleasant atmosphere) overlooking the harbor. The chefs do their thing right in the room where you dine. (207) 775-2717

• Flatbread Company — Portland
  Delicious all-natural gourmet pizza from wood-fired clay ovens gives this place its name. Its location, at 72 Commercial Street, gives it one of the best waterfront views in Portland. (207) 772-8777

• Diamond's Edge — Diamond Island, Casco Bay
  A unique island setting makes the food irrelevant...but it's good anyway. Moderate-to-expensive. Go by boat or ferry. (207) 766-5804

• Royal River Grillhouse — Yarmouth
  Casual dining with a view of the water from every seat in the house. Seafood, steak, poultry and game prepared on a wood fire. (207) 846-1226

• Becky's on Hobson's Wharf — Portland
  If it's a hearty breakfast you want, try this little diner on the waterfront on Commercial Street. Everything you can think of up through blueberry pancakes and French toast, plus fresh fruit bowls. Lunch, too. (207) 773-7070

Western Mountains & Lakes

• Center Lovell Inn — Center Lovell
  A varied menu served indoors or on the porch. Breakfast, too. Moderate-to-expensive. (207) 925-1575

• The Olde House — Raymond
  A 1790 landmark with candlelight dining, extensive and varied menu. Moderate. (207) 655-7841

• Oxford House Inn — Fryeburg
  Varied menu with many delightful, sophisticated specials. The rear dining room of the 1913 inn offers sweeping mountain views. Moderate-to-expensive. (207) 935-3442, 1-800-261-7206

• Bray's Brew Pub — Naples
  Seafood, beef and more served up with the house brew, in which mussels are stewed. Moderate. (207) 693-6806

• Lake House — Waterford
  Informal atmosphere with outstanding food served with flair. Moderate. (207) 583-4182, 1-800-223-4182

• Bethel Inn & Country Club — Bethel
Fine dining in an elegant atmosphere overlooking the golf course. Moderate-to-expensive. (207) 824-2175

• Sunday River Brewing Company — North Bethel
Pizza, burgers, soups, salads and a variety of brews served between kettles and tanks. Inexpensive. (207) 824-4ALE

• Kawanhee Inn — Weld
Candlelight dining in a traditional mountain lodge setting overlooking Webb Lake. Moderate. (207) 585-2000

• Rangeley Inn — Rangeley
Elegant dining in a fitting, old-fashioned hotel dining room. Moderate-to-expensive. (207) 864-3341

• One Stanley Avenue — Kingfield
Cocktails in the parlor, elegant dining in two small rooms. Sophisticated menu with delightful specials. Expensive. (207) 265-5541

• Longfellow Restaurant & Riverside Lounge — Kingfield
A step back into the town's past with good, solid menu. Inexpensive-to-moderate. (207) 265-4394

Midcoast

• The Dolphin Marina — South Harpswell
Chowder, lobster stew, homemade desserts and a view of the harbor. A local favorite. Go by car or boat. Inexpensive. (207) 833-6000

• Lobster Village at Mackerel Cove — Bailey Island
Specializing in lobster and seafood, an informal atmosphere at the water's edge. Breakfast, lunch and dinner daily. (207) 833-6656

• The Robinhood Free Meetinghouse — Robinhood
First-class dining in a beautiful 1855 church refurbished to provide a unique culinary experience. Moderate-to-expensive. (207) 371-2188

• Le Garage — Wiscasset
Try to get a table on the porch, then enjoy seafood, steaks and veggie specialties overlooking the river. Moderate. (207) 882-5409

• Lobsterman's Wharf — East Boothbay
   Far enough off the beaten track to attract locals. Enjoy moderately-priced seafood, pastas and pizza (and lobster) in a waterside setting. (207) 633-3443

• Ocean Point Inn — East Boothbay
   Three informal dining rooms with water views. Steaks, salmon, chicken, crab cakes. (207) 633-4200

• Cabbage Island Clambake — Boothbay Harbor
   The good ship Argo leaves Fisherman's Wharf daily bound for Cabbage Island, where an old-fashioned clambake awaits in a rustic lodge. (207) 633-7200

• The Newcastle Inn — Newcastle
   Sophisticated menu, candlelit romantic atmosphere, a memorable dining experience. Expensive. (207) 563-5685

• Gosnold Arms — New Harbor
   Fresh local seafood served straight up, not fancy. Broiled salmon steak, casseroles, fried seafood. Moderate. (207) 677-3727

• Bradley Inn — New Harbor
   Good food (some special) in a nautical atmosphere. Live jazz and folk music on Friday and Saturday nights. Moderate-to-expensive. (207) 677-2105, 1-800-942-5560

• Anchor Inn — Round Pond
   Overlooking the harbor of a small fishing village. Seafood served Italian style. Moderate. (207) 529-5584

• Moody's Diner — Waldoboro
   Classic diner fare in a classic diner atmosphere, clean and welcoming. Try the pies. In fact, don't miss the pies. Inexpensive. (207) 832-7468

• Osier's Wharf — South Bristol
   Overlooking the lobsterman's harbor, upstairs and serving plain and good stuff. Inexpensive. (207) 644-8101

• The Harpoon — Port Clyde
   Fresh seafood with some pleasant surprises. Inexpensive. (207) 372-6304

• East Wind Inn — Tenants Harbor
Local seafood served overlooking the harbor. Extensive menu. Moderate.
(207) 372-6366

• Cod End — Tenants Harbor
This fish shop has a pleasant eatery, too, with tables outside as well as in.
Right on the harbor. Inexpensive. (207) 372-6782

• Miller's Lobster Company — Spruce Head
Local favorite, right on the harbor, with fresh seafood, locally caught.
Inexpensive. (207) 594-7406

• Marcel's — Rockport
Almost formal dining at the elegant Samoset Resort. The wine list is a recipient
of Wine Spectator's "Award of Excellence." Classics served with flair. Moderate-
to-expensive. (207) 594-0774

• The Sail Loft — Rockport
Seafood specialties overlooking the harbor and boatyard. Moderate-to-
expensive. (207) 236-2330

• Chez Michel — Lincolnville Beach
Good food with a French flair served inside or out. Inexpensive-to-moderate.
(207) 789-5600

• Cork-Bistro, Wine Café & Gallery — Camden
The wine list may be enough to draw you into crowded Camden. Pleasant
with some nice menu surprises. Moderate-to-expensive. (207) 230-0533

• Blue Harbor House — Camden
Limited menu (multi-course, candle-lit dinner, or old-fashioned Down East
lobster feed — $35) in charming 1810 Inn. Reservations required. (207) 236-3196.

• Marquis at the Belmont — Camden
"Unpretentious elegance and innovative cuisine." A favorite of the locals
when a fine dinner out is on the menu. (207) 236-8053 or 1-800-238-8053.
www.thebelmontinn.com

• Hartstone Inn — Camden
A charming 1835 Mansard-style home is the setting for this charming inn,
which features beautifully-decorated rooms, some with claw-foot soaking tubs,

fireplaces and canopy beds. Elegant dining with an international flair supervised by award-winning Chef Michael. The menu changes seasonally; the well-stocked wine cellar remains constant. Featured in Food & Wine and Gourmet magazines, and a Yankee Magazine Editor's Pick.
41 Elm Street, Camden, ME 04843
(207) 236-4259 or 1-800-788-4823
www.hartstoneinn.com
email: info@hartstoneinn.com

• Rhumb Line — Searsport
  Enjoy a cocktail in the parlor, then get treated to good food and fine wine in the dining room. Moderate-to-expensive. (207) 548-2600

Down East

• Riverside Café — Ellsworth
  Sisters Beth and Barbara pride themselves on fresh food, from breakfast (served all day) to dinner in a casual, open atmosphere. Vegetarian menu, too. Inexpensive. (207) 667-7220

• Maidee's — Ellsworth
  Upscale Chinese fare. A favorite after-theater hangout for dessert right across the street from the Grand Auditorium. (207) 667-6554.

• Hilltop House — Ellsworth
  Where the locals go — for everything from pizza to a steak or lobster dinner. (207) 667-9368.

• McCleod's — Bucksport
  Unpretentious, but good, fresh food — from fish to ribs to homemade soups and desserts. A local favorite. Water views. Inexpensive-to-moderate. (207) 469-3963

• Reading Room — Bar Harbor
  Luxurious dining overlooking Frenchman's Bay. Sunday brunch, too. Moderate-to-expensive. (207) 288-3351 or 1-800-248-3351

• The Rose Garden/Bluenose Inn — Bar Harbor
  An award-winning four-diamond dining experience that many feel is among the very best. Expensive. (207) 288-3348 or 1-800-445-4077

• George's — Bar Harbor
Mediterranean and international cuisine, in its 25th year. Weekend entertainment, too. Moderate-to-expensive. (207) 288-4505

• Surry Inn — Surry
A favorite among locals for good food, reasonably priced. Moderate. (207) 667-5091

• The Lookout — North Brooklin
Ask for a table on the porch so you can enjoy the spectacular views along with good food. Moderate. (207) 359-2188

• Oakland House — Brooksville
Huge portions, good food, moderate prices. (207) 359-8521

• Castine Inn — Castine
Considered THE dining spot in Castine, with an extensive and sophisticated menu and special ambiance. Moderate-to-expensive. (207) 326-4365

• Bah's Bake House — Castine
A nice little deli with great breads, soups, sandwiches. (207) 326-9510

• Goose Cove Lodge — Sunset
Spectacular food in a spectacular setting. Expensive. (207) 348-2508 or 1-800-728-1963

• Jordan Pond House — Seal Harbor
A rebuilt 1870s landmark offering an extensive and appealing menu in a pleasant atmosphere. Moderate. (207) 276-3316

• The Burning Tree — Otter Creek
Fresh fish and organically-grown produce, nicely prepared and presented inside or on the porch. Moderate. (207) 288-9331

• XYZ Restaurant & Gallery — Manset
Good Mexican food, believe it or not. Inexpensive. (207) 244-5221

• The Islesford Dock — Little Cranberry Island
Local seafood and produce well prepared and presented right at the dock. Enjoy the sunset over Mount Desert Island. Moderate. (207) 244-7494

• Thurston's Lobster Pound — Bernard
On the water overlooking Bass Harbor. Lobster as it's supposed to be, plus more. Inexpensive. (207) 244-7600

• Le Domaine — Hancock
French cuisine done right in a European ambiance. Expensive. (207) 422-3395

• Helen's — Machias
Overlooking the Machias River. Family restaurant specializing in steaks and salads. Famous for its homemade pies. (207) 255-8422/

• The Blue Bird Ranch — Machias
Fresh seafood, steaks, pasta — a local hangout for breakfast, lunch and dinner. (207) 255-3351.

• Seafarer's Wife — Jonesport
Menu ranges from vegetarian specialties to a baked seafood platter with shrimp, lobster, halibut and scallops. Moderate. (207) 497-2365

• Harbor House on Sawyer Cove — Jonesport
Lobster and crabmeat, but more, all served inside or on the porch overlooking the water. Inexpensive. (207) 497-5417

• The Waterside Inn — Lubec
Good lobster, crab rolls, chowder in an old sardine-processing plant. Outdoor tables. Moderate. (207) 733-2500

• Eastport Lobster & Fish House — Eastport
Formal dining upstairs, informal pub downstairs, both good. Moderate. (207) 853-9663

• The Chandler House — Calais
Specializing in seafood, but good prime rib, too. Moderate. (207) 454-7922

The Islands

• The Periwinkle — Monhegan Island
Breakfast, lunch and dinner, water views, varied menu. Inexpensive-to-moderate. (207) 594-5432

• The Island Inn — Monhegan Island
Varied menu with many special dishes. Moderate-to-expensive. (207) 596-0371 email: islandin@midcoast.com

• Candlepin Lodge — Vinalhaven
The island's hub, a bowling alley with booths and soda fountain on one side and dining room on the other. Local catch, including steamers. Inexpensive-to-moderate. (207) 863-2730

• Pilgrim's Inn — Deer Isle
Join other guests on the deck for hors d'oeuvres and cocktails, then move on to the five-course dinner inside. Special. Expensive. (207) 348-6615

Kennebec & Moose River Valleys

• Old Mill Pub — Skowhegan
Dine overlooking the Kennebec River — even on the porch, which puts you right over it. Casual atmosphere, varied menu from burgers to full dinners. (207) 474-6627

• Moose Point Tavern — Jackman
On the shore of Big Wood Lake. Varied menu. Inexpensive. (207) 668-4012

• Loon's Look-Out — Jackman
A small Italian restaurant with good food. Take-out available. Inexpensive. (207) 668-3351

Moosehead Lake & Katahdin

• Greenville Inn — Greenville
A sophisticated menu, well-executed and served. Moderate-to-expensive. (207) 695-2206, 1-800-695-6000

• Blair Hill Inn — Greenville
Fine dining with the best views of Moosehead Lake imaginable. For that "special occasion." (207) 695-0224

Ferries

The Ferry Elizabeth Ann, courtesy of Monhegan Boat Line, Port Clyde

Maine's thousands of coastal islands are a prime way to enjoy the state — to see the pristine new land much the way the European explorers first saw it centuries ago.

The islands have no interstate highways, few paved roads (some have neither cars nor roads) and even fewer bridges. Nonetheless, many are accessible even to those who don't happen to have a cruising vessel to get around on their own.

Here's a great place to start.

Greater Portland

Casco Bay Lines

• Mailboat Run

A three-hour tour of the islands of Casco Bay. 7:45am Mon-Fri (summer only), 10am daily, 2:15pm daily (summer only), 2:45pm daily. $10.75, $9.50 for seniors, $5 for children.

• Bailey Island Cruise

A six-hour cruise to Casco Bay's premier historical sites and vistas. 10am from Portland, 2pm from Bailey Island. $15.50, $14 for seniors, $7.50 for children.

• Bailey Island Nature Watch

Two hours. 12 noon from Bailey Island. $9.50, $8 for seniors, $4 for children

• Diamond Pass
    Two-hour cruise around Little Diamond, Great Diamond and Peaks islands. 11am, 1:15pm, 3:15pm (11am off-season). $9.50, $8 for seniors, $4 for children.

• Sunrise on the Bay
    Two hours, 30 minutes. 5:05am Mon-Fri. $10.75, $9.50 for seniors, $5 for children.

• Sunset Run
    Two hours, 30 minutes. 5:45pm daily. $10.75, $9.50 for seniors, $5 for children.

• Moonlight Run
    Two hours. 9:15pm. $9.50, $8 for seniors, $4 for children.

• Music Cruises
    Scheduled throughout the summer with various bands; call for details. Also available: ferries to Chebeague Island, Cliff Island and Long Island. The Casco Bay Lines terminal is located at the corner of Commercial and Franklin streets in Portland. Take I-95 to I-295; take exit 7 and continue on Franklin Street to end. (207) 774-7871
email: information@cascobaylines.com

Midcoast

Maine State Ferry Service

• Matinicus Island, Vinalhaven and North Haven from Rockland
$9*, $4 for children; $26 for cars** (plus $2/foot additional for larger vehicles)

• Islesboro from Lincolnville
$4.50, $2 for children; $13 for cars (plus $1/foot for larger vehicles)

• Swans Island and Frenchboro from Bass Harbor
$6, $3 for children; $18 for cars (plus $2/foot for larger vehicles)

*Rates quoted are round-trip fares.
**Advance reservations for vehicles are recommended.
Call for directions to terminal locations. (207) 596-2202
website: www.state.me.us/mdot/opt/ferry/feryinfo.htm

Suggestion: Don't miss the last ferry back unless you have reservations for a place to stay on the islands — it's a long wait and an even longer swim.

Monhegan Boat Line

• Thomaston to Monhegan Island
   Cruise aboard the Laura B or the Elizabeth Ann to fabled Monhegan Island. Several departures daily — the trip takes between 50 and 70 minutes.

• Port Clyde to Monhegan Island
   The Laura B and the Elizabeth Ann depart from Port Clyde, too.
Reservations are required. No vehicles. $16 one way, $27 round trip; children 2-12 $14 round trip; pets $2 round trip. (These boats are also available for charters and excursions.)
(207) 372-8848
www.monheganboat.com
email: barstow@monheganboat.com

Balmy Days Cruises

• Boothbay Harbor to Monhegan Island
   The Balmy Days II departs twice daily during the summer, less frequently in the spring and fall. $30 round trip, $18 for children. (This firm also offers pleasure cruises.)
(207) 633-2284 or 1-800-298-2284
45 Commercial Street, Boothbay Harbor, ME 04538
www.anchorwatch.com/balmy
email: diane@lincoln.midcoast.com

Down East

East Coast Ferries

• Deer Island to Campobello (and beyond to New Brunswick)

• Deer Island to Eastport
   Frequent departures, vehicles welcomed. Passage ranges from $2 (passengers only) to $13 (car and driver) to $45 (motor coaches).
(506) 747-2159
P.O. Box 301, Lord's Cove, Deer Island, N.B. E5V 1W2

www.eastcoastferries.nb.ca
email: info@eastcoastferries.nb.ca

Isle au Haut Ferries

Daily excursions aboard Miss Lizzie on Penobscot Bay between Stonington and Isle au Haut. Visits to Duck Harbor, also. Several trips daily. No vehicles. (Pleasure cruises also available.)
(207) 367-5193
www.isleauhaut.com
email: staige@together.net

Cranberry Cove Boating Company

Frequent daily service between Southwest Harbor and the islands of Great Cranberry, Islesford and Suttons. No vehicles. (207) 244-5882, (207) 460-3977 (boat)
www.rootsweb.com
email: cliebow@acadia.net

Bay Ferries

The Bay Ferries' Cat is the fastest car ferry in North America, and carries up to 900 passengers and 240 vehicles at speeds up to 90Km/hr between Bar Harbor and Yarmouth, Nova Scotia, cutting travel time to about two hours and 30 minutes. Call for reservations, rates and other information.
(207) 288-3395, 1-888-249SAIL
www.canadaferry.com

Note: Also see our section on Boats and Boating; there are a number of wonderful opportunities to visit many of Maine's islands — even the uninhabited ones — aboard other watercraft.

Festivals & Fairs

Fryeburg Fair, by John Brough

Festivals and fairs may be one of the most challenging ways to avoid crowds and tourists in Maine, but many are far from the beaten track, and are frequented more by Mainers than visitors from away. Regardless, they are one of better ways to enjoy many of the things that make this great state a most enjoyable place to live as well as visit.

Festivals

Southern Coastal

• Harvestfest — York — October
  Food, music, antiques auction, chocolate festival, chowder, lobster, crafts, fun for the whole family under the tent. Southern York County's premiere event. (207) 363-4422

• Yarmouth Clam Festival — July
  Clams every which way, plus races, parade, games, entertainment. (207) 846-3984

• Capricio — Ogunquit — September
Celebration of the performing arts, with concerts, theater, even a performance by the Portland Ballet. (207) 646-6170

Western Mountains & Lakes

• Four Feathers Native American Festival and Pow-wow — Leeds — July
Native American dancers, crafts, artisans representing tribes from South and Central America as well as North America.
(207) 872-5754

• Great Falls Balloon Festival — Lewiston-Auburn — August
One of New England's biggest hot-air balloon gatherings. Concerts, crafts and trade exhibits, children's activities.
(207) 783-2249

Midcoast

• Schooner Day — Rockland — July
The spectacular Schooner Parade of Sail in Rockland Harbor takes place off the Rockland Breakwater. The best news about this event is that it can be enjoyed from almost anywhere along the Rockland Harbor waterfront; there are many uncrowded sites from which to enjoy the show (although getting into Rockland during the festival is a challenge, as is finding accommodations). The tall ships are open to visitors, and boat rides and sailing adventures are offered in abundance.
For more information, call (207) 596-0376. For help with lodging, call the Rockland-Thomaston Chamber of Commerce at 1-800-562-2529.
www.midcoast.com

• North Atlantic Blues Festival — Rockland — July
Top blues bands and performers plus a Saturday nightclub "crawl."
(207) 236-7660

• Friendship Sloop Days — Rockland — July
If you love Friendship sloops (and how could you not?), this one's for you. Regatta, demonstrations and the opportunity to see these beautiful boats up close and personal.
(207) 832-4818

• Maine Lobster Festival — Rockland — August
If lobster is your thing, this is the place to enjoy it to the fullest. Indeed, you

won't find a lobster dinner for under $10 anywhere else. Enjoy yours amid pageants, parades, exhibitions, art exhibits, crafts shows, music and entertainment, a road race, boat rides, open houses and more (e.g., the Great International Lobster Crate Race).
(207) 596-0376 or 1-800-LOB-CLAW.
www.mainelobsterfestival.com

• Maine Festival of the Arts — Brunswick — August
The Annual Maine Festival of the Arts is staged over three days at Thomas Point Beach in Brunswick. A juried art exhibition, crafts sale, interactive art activities and performances of the lively arts on seven stage venues — music, dance, comedy — a celebration of the creativity of Mainers.
(207) 772-9012 or 1-800-639-4212 for more information.
www.mainearts.org/festhome.html

• Maine Antiques Festival — Union — August
The Annual Maine Antiques Festival is a tradition in the rural town of Union. At the fairgrounds. Early buying during set-up after 2pm Friday.
(207) 563-1013
www.maineantiquefest.com
email: cpishows@lincoln.midcoast.com

• Maine Storytellers Festival
The dates and venues for the Storytellers Festival are flexible, but this one is worth checking into — 10 evenings of humor and storytelling on stages from Kennebunk to Camden. A fun way to learn about Maine's unique heritage. (207) 743-0757
http://storytellers.maine.com
email: StoryTellers@Maine.com

• North Atlantic Folk Festival — Rockland — August
Big-name performers.
(207) 236-7660

• Windjammer Weekend — Camden — August-September
One of the largest gatherings of Maine windjammers. Music, the boat parade, film exhibitions and fireworks display.
(207) 236-4404

• Maine Apple Day — Unity — November
Apple growers and apple lovers join for a celebration that includes tasting,

sampling and even a pie-baking contest. Well-known Maine personalities and chefs judge the entries and award the prizes.
(207) 933-2100

Down East

• Downeast Folk Music Festival — Bar Harbor — July
   Traditional folk music, plus bagpipes, harps, whistles and dulcimers. Open-mike opportunities, too.
(207) 288-5653

• Native American Festival — Bar Harbor — July
   A celebration of Native American culture, arts and crafts, demonstrations, traditional food. At College of the Atlantic campus.
(207) 288-3519

• Schoodic Arts Festival — Prospect Harbor — August
   An annual two-week celebration of dance, theater, music, visual arts, writing and crafts. A full day of Maine storytelling, too. Many performances are free. Everything from African drums and mime to classical music and ballet.
P.O. Box 106, Prospect Harbor, ME 04669
1-866-751-2787
www.schoodicarts.org
email: MaryLaury@acadia.net

• Wild Blueberry Festival — Machias — August
   A real old-fashioned country good time as the blueberry harvest is celebrated where (they claim) 85 percent of the world's blueberries are grown. Parade, fish fry, road race and all the best blueberry foods you can eat (including a blueberry-pie-eating contest).
www.nemaine.com/blueberry

Kennebec & Moose River Valleys

• Maine International Film Festival — Waterville — July
   American and foreign classics, plus cutting-edge new releases.
(207) 861-8138
www.miff.org
email: info@miff.org

Moosehead Lake & Katahdin

• Wooden Canoe Festival — Millinocket — August
   The Sixth Annual Festival will feature the wooden canoe show, plus displays, workshops, a parade and fly-tying demonstrations.
(207) 783-4443

Far North

• Maine Potato Blossom Festival — Fort Fairfield — July
   Parade, floats, food, music, antique-car show, fireworks — fun for the whole family. Some think the crowning of the Maine Potato Queen is the highlight; others may prefer the mashed-potato-wrestling event.
   Call the Fort Fairfield Chamber of Commerce for event schedule and more information at (207) 472-3802.
   www.fortfairfield.org
   email: ffcc@mfx.net

Fairs

   Maine's Fairs — small, country and relaxed (the larger ones are so noted) — are a special glimpse into "life as it should be" for many, particularly those in residence. Visitors are welcome, of course, and you may well find yourself feeling like a native as you enjoy the livestock, produce, crafts, contests, racing, midways and entertainment.

   They are listed here in chronological order, July through the fall.

✦✦✦ *July* ✦✦✦
• Houlton
• Ossipee Valley Fair, Hiram
• Pittston Fair
• World's Fair, Waterford
• Bangor State Fair
• Northern Maine Fair, Presque Isle

✦✦✦ *August* ✦✦✦
• Monmouth Fair
• Athens Fair
• Topsham Fair

• Skowhegan State Fair
• Union Fair
    Carnival, crafts, antique autos, harness racing, tractor-pulling contest, children's pig scrambles, exhibits, food, music and entertainment, all topped with fireworks.
(207) 785-3281 (off-season, (207) 236-8009).
www.union-fair.com
• Piscataquis Valley Fair, Dover-Foxcroft
• Acton Fair
• Windsor Fair
    Harness racing, woodman's day, farm products and animal exhibits, horse-pulling and tractor-pulling contests, antique tractors, carnival attractions, food, music, entertainment.
(207) 549-5249.
www.windsorfair.com
• Blue Hill Fair
• Springfield Fair

◆◆◆ *September* ◆◆◆
• Clinton Lions
• Litchfield Fair
• Oxford Fair
• New Portland Fair
• Farmington Fair
• Common Ground Fair, Unity
    Entertainment, exhibits, shows, contests (i.e., fiddle contest, foot race and the Harry Truman Manure Pitch-off), horse-team demonstrations, folk arts, forestry exhibits, learning opportunities (especially via MOFGA, the Maine Organic Farmers and Gardeners Association) and, of course, food. A celebration of rural living.
www.mofga.org
• Cumberland Fair
• Fryeburg Fair
    This is no place to avoid crowds (this fair attracts many thousands from far and wide for eight days), but it's special and fun, with attractions for anyone who enjoys rural life.
(207) 268-4631
www.getrealmaine.com/fairs/index.html
email: mbonin2404@ctel.net

Native Foods

Portland Public Market, by Dick Balkite

Most people who visit Maine are seeking to experience its unmatched beauty, the serenity of the woods, the spectacular ocean vistas...and many can't resist the taste of lobster.

There's much more, however, that makes the taste of Maine something very special. Here are some examples:

Farmers' Markets

Maine's farms, as much as its seacoast and forests, have for centuries been the essence of this great corner of the country. There are no huge "corporate" farms or mega-producers such as you would find in the Midwest or Southwest. There is, however, a landscape punctuated by small family farms that produce a wide variety of wholesome, tasty foods. And they're here for you to sample at the state's traditional farmers' markets, which dot the landscape throughout the harvesting season. Many Mainers have long preferred this source of native produce of all kinds because the minimal time between field and table virtually guarantees freshness that you just can't get any way other than growing your own.

Southern Coastal

• Biddeford Public Market
Chevenell Park on Main Street. Saturday
(207) 282-9926

• Saco Farmers' and Artisans' Market
Saco Valley Shopping Center on Spring Street. Wednesday, Saturday
(207) 929-5318
email: snellfrm@cybertours.com

• Springvale/Sanford Farmers' Market
Route 109 at Route 11A in Sanford. Wednesday, Saturday
(207) 324-0331
email: annie@psouth.net

Greater Portland

• Portland Farmers' Market
Monument Square on Wednesday; Deering Oaks Park on Saturday.
(207) 883-5750
email: hfff@maine.rr.com

• Portland Public Market
Corner of Cumberland and Preble. A visit here is always a special treat; you could argue that the ambiance is equal to the food, which is saying something. Daily, year-round
(207) 228-2001
www.portlandmarket.com
email: mkoerick@portlandmarket.com

• Westbrook Farmers' Market
Dunn Street corner of Riverbank Park. Friday
(207) 854-9105
email: meddy@westbrook.me.us

Western Mountains & Lakes

• Auburn Farmers' Market
Porteous rear lot, Turner Street side. Thursday and Saturday
(207) 336-2411

• Bethel Farmers' Market
Bethel Health Center, Railroad Street. Saturday
(207) 836-3606

• Bridgton Farmers' Market
Side lot at Crafters Outlet on Route 302. Saturday

• Naples Farmers' Market
Village Green off Route 302. Thursday
(207) 642-5161

• Norway Farmers' Market
Main Street at Cottage Street. Friday
(207) 539-4848

• Phillips Farmers' Market
Main Street. Saturday
(207) 639-4021
email: dbuckley@sad58.k12.me.us

• Sandy River Farmers' Market — Farmington
Better Living Center on Front Street
(207) 265-2248

Midcoast

• Bath Farmers' Market
Commercial Street at Waterfront Park. Thursday and Saturday
(207) 586-5067
email: jlmercer@lincoln.midcoast.com

• Belfast Winter Farmers' Market
Greenhouse at Belfast Agway, Route 1. Thursday and Saturday
(207) 338-5084
http://midcoast.com/-hunter/belfastfarmmkt
email: nif@acadia.net

• Boothbay Farmers' Market
Meadowbrook Mall on Route 27. Thursday
(207) 737-8834
email: veggies@agate.net

• Brunswick Farmers' Market
Brunswick Mall on Maine Street. Tuesday, Friday, Saturday
Crystal Springs on Pleasant Hill Road. Saturday only
(207) 729-6108
email: catalog@lilacs.com

• Camden Farmers' Market
Colcord Street across from Tibbets Industries. Wednesday and Saturday
(207) 273-2809
www.midcoast.com/-hunter/CamdenFarmMkt/index.html
email: jbarnstein@aol.com

• Cumberland Farmers' Market
Greeley Green on Main Street. Saturday
(207) 829-5588

• Damariscotta Area Farmers' Market
Business Route 1 at Belvedere Road. Monday and Friday
(207) 563-1076
email: mushroom@lincoln.midcoast.com

• Phippsburg Town Market
Town Hall, Route 209. Saturday
(207) 389-1597

• Rockland Farmers' Market
Downtown at the waterfront. Thursday
(207) 563-1076
email: mushroom@lincoln.midcoast.com

• Unity Market Day-Farmers' Market
Route 139 at School Street. Saturday
(207) 948-9005
www.members.mint.net/troberts

Down East

• Brewer Farmers' Market
Brewer Auditorium on Wilson Street. Tuesday through Saturday
(207) 948-5724
email: joyce.benson@state.me.us

• Bucksport Farmers' Market
Post Office parking lot on Lower Main Street. Thursday
(207) 469-0015
email: Beckbaker3546646@cs.com

• Stonington/Deer Isle Farmers' Market
Congregational Church parking lot. Friday
(207) 326-4741
email: sunsetacres@acadia.net

• Eden Farmers' Market — Bar Harbor
YMCA parking lot, Main Street. Sunday
(207) 288-3907
email: mgerald@acadia.net

• Ellsworth Farmers' Market
High Street at Foster Street. Thursday and Saturday

• Hampden Farmers' Market
Barco Credit Union parking lot on Western Avenue. Saturday
(207) 862-3079

• Machias Valley Farmers' Market — Machias
Route 1 at the dike. Saturday
(207) 638-2664
email: rcvarin@rivah.net

• Northeast Harbor Farmers' Market
Old high school. Thursday
(207) 288-4930
email: mgerald@acadia.net

• Sunrise County Farmers' Market (Calais, Eastport, Perry)
Union Street across for Information Bureau in Calais on Tuesday; Next to Ray's Mustard on Washington Street in Eastport on Thursday; Perry Municipal Building parking lot on Route 1 in Perry on Saturday.
(207) 454-7496

Kennebec & Moose River Valleys

• Augusta Farmers' Market
Turnpike Mall, Western Avenue. Accommodations for special parties and events;
40' x 60' tent, volleyball, shuffleboard and horseshoe courts, too. Wednesday and
Saturday
(207) 549-5112
email: broacres@midcoast.com

• Fairfield Farmers' Market
Water Street off Main Street. Wednesday, Saturday
(207) 453-4280

• Hallowell Sunday Market
Water Street (Route 201) opposite boat landing. Sunday
(207) 622-6582
email: npmcg@hotmail.com

• Pittsfield Farmers' Market
Hathorn Park on Hatland Avenue. Monday and Thursday
(207) 487-5056
www.members.mint.net/troberts/PIT
email: troberts@mint.net

• Skowhegan Organic Farmers' Market
Next to Information Center on Russell Street. Saturday
(207) 683-2044
www.skoworganicmarket@yahoo.com
email: billib66@yahoo.com

• Winthrop Farmers' Market
Downtown municipal parking lot. Tuesday and Saturday
(207) 395-4244
www.camarkets.com
email: winfarmkt@hotmail.com

Moosehead Lake & Katahdin

• Dexter Farmers' Market
Route 7 between Dexter and Corinna. Friday
(207) 924-7900

Far   North

• Houlton Farmers' Market
Route 1 South off I-95 next to McDonald's. Open every day
(207) 794-8306

• Madawaska Marketplace
Main Street and 11th Avenue. Saturday
(207) 895-5234
email: jskylandia@ncil.net

• Presque Isle Farmers' Market
Aroostook Center Mall on Route 1. Saturday
(207) 896-5860

Fruits, berries, vegetables and flowers

There are some 150 farms throughout Maine that invite you to "pick your own." For their locations, phone numbers and seasons, go to www.mainefoodandfarms.com
or email maine.food@state.me.us

Specialty and gourmet Maine food products
You can also get information on some of Maine's most delectable foods, including where to get them (and how to link with mail-order sites) at www.mainefoods.org.

Gardens & Flowers

Garden walk, courtesy of McLaughlin Foundation

Maine's winters are notably harsh and long, but come the spring and summer, Maine explodes with a bounty of gardens and wildflowers. Gardens in Maine are unique; they tend to be modest in scale and limited to a short season but are, nevertheless, a wonder to behold. Our soil, landscape and North Atlantic proximity combine to produce plentiful, vibrant and colorful plant life. It seems as if everyone in Maine has a small fruit, vegetable, flower or herb garden — perhaps an annual affirmation of our good life.

Mainers also keenly appreciate the botanical wonders that are the result of long cultivation and special horticultural talent. We are gifted with many public gardens throughout the state in a wide variety of settings, from coastal island, to rural farm, to urban park. Some of them are highly stylized, others informal, still others have historical significance and some are solely the work of nature. All are inviting and uplifting so please enjoy them.

Southern Coastal

• Celia Thaxter's Garden — Appledore Island, Isles of Shoals

Way back in 1614 Captain John Smith noted the Isles of Shoals, the cluster of small islands eight miles from the mainland where Maine and New Hampshire meet. They were probably named for the once-great number of fishes that schooled (or shoaled) around them. Appledore, the largest at 95 acres, is home to the tiniest but perhaps most beloved garden in Maine. The original garden was the creation of Celia Laighton Thaxter (1835-1894), hostess extraordinaire, poet, artist, gardener and author of An Island Garden. Celia presided over an amazing literary salon that attracted the likes of Ralph Waldo Emerson, Nathaniel Hawthorne, Richard Henry Dana, Henry Wadsworth Longfellow, John Greenleaf Whittier and Thomas Bailey Aldrich.

In the 1970s the Shoals Marine Laboratory, the Rye Beach Little Boar's Head Garden Club, Cornell Plantations and other friends authentically reconstructed Celia's 15-by-50 foot garden. Today you can again experience the nasturtiums, white lilies, petunias, sweet william, foxgove, rugosa roses and other flowers she painstakingly tended in a rugged and challenging environment.

Open only on Wednesdays, by reservation, for most of the summer. Day trips only; toilet facilities but no food accommodations. Bring your lunch and have a picnic looking out to sea.
(607) 255-3717
shoals-lab@cornell.lab
www.sml.cornell.edu
Ferry info: www.islesofshoals.com

• Hamilton House — South Berwick
The state's best example of a Victorian-era garden. The Georgian mansion is surrounded by a circa 1898 colonial revival garden restored in the late 1990s. Manicured beds with a beautiful array of annuals and perennials overlooking Salmon Falls River. Self-guided garden tour with a map and historic photos. A National Historic Landmark with 35 acres and walking trails. Open June through mid-Oct., dawn to dusk.
40 Vaughn's Lane, South Berwick, ME 03908
(207) 384-2454
www.spnea.org/visit/homes/hamilton.htm

• Marrett House — Standish
Home purchased in 1796 by recent Harvard graduate Daniel Marrett, who went on to become the town's most prominent citizen. Much of the furnishings and interior preserved as relics of the past. The Marrett sisters' perennials garden of the 1920s and 30s has been restored.
Route 25 (I95 to exit 8, follow Rt. 25 to center of Standish)
Standish, ME 04084
(207) 642-3032
www.spnea.org/visit/homes/marrett.htm

• St. Anthony's Shire and Franciscan Monastery — Kennebunkport

Former estate designed in 1906-1917 by the Olmsted brothers, sons of landscape design pioneer, Fredrick Law Olmsted. Twenty-five acres of beautiful grounds under a canopy of trees with walks, paths and a great rhododendron display that peaks in June. The monastery overlooks a marsh and the Kennebunk River. A wonderful place to worship or meditate in beautiful surroundings.

Beach Avenue, Kennebunkport, ME

(207) 967-2011

Greater Portland

• Gilsland Farm Sanctuary — Falmouth

A 65-acre Audubon Society retreat with wildflower meadows, peony gardens, woods and marsh along the Presumpscot Estuary. The sharp eye will also find a myriad of wildlife. An opportunity for seclusion and relaxation only a few miles from bustling downtown Portland.

(207) 781-2330

118 Rt. 1, Falmouth, ME

www.maineaudubon.org

• Wadsworth-Longfellow House & Gardens — Portland

This 1785 house, now a museum, was the childhood home of Henry Wadsworth Longfellow. The adjacent Longfellow Gardens were laid out in 1920s and restored in the mid 1990s and are a National Historic Landmark. Pick up a copy of Longfellow's Evangeline to read in the gardens and steep yourself in the Acadian culture that is so much a part of Maine.

(207) 774-1822

487 Congress Street, Portland, ME

www.mainehistory.com

• Deering Oaks Rose Garden — Portland

Fifty-one acres designed by William Goodwin in 1870. Part of the Portland Parks System and on the National Register of Historic Places. Oaks (some thought to be over 200 years old), pines and spruce provide a high canopy for over 600 species, including hybrid tea roses. Stroll the recently-built pedestrian walkway and be sure to see the newly-planted ravine and spray pool.

At Deering and Forest Avenue, Portland, ME

(207) 874-8300

• Tate House Museum Herb Garden — Portland
Do not miss seeing this museum and herb garden if you are interested in our colonial past. The house was built in 1755 for Capt. George Tate following his arrival in the colonies to act as Senior Mast Agent for the British Navy. It's the only pre-Revolutionary home in Portland open to the public. The garden contains more than 50 herbs that correspond to varieties the Tate family may have used while they occupied the house from 1755 to 1803. The property is own by The Colonial Dames of America and was designated a National Landmark in 1972. The house is open select hours and days June through October.
1270 Westbrook St., Portland, ME
(207) 774 -6177
www.tatehouse.org
tate@gwi.net

Western Mountains & Lakes

• The McLaughlin Foundation Garden & Horticultural Center — South Paris
This is truly a very special place. It was voted Best Garden In Maine (July '98 and '00, MaineTimes Readers Poll) and Favorite Public Garden in New England ('98 and '99, People, Places and Plants Magazine). This 1840s farmstead with a two-acre perennial garden and arboretum provides an opportunity to view extensive collections of lilac, wildflower, hosta, sedum, sempervivum, daylily, astilbe and iris. For 60 years gardeners and garden lovers have been welcome to enter the garden. It is the legacy of Bernard McLaughlin, who began the garden in 1936 while working in a South Paris grocery store and gardened in his spare time until retiring in 1967. From that point until his recent death he devoted his full energies to the garden, purposefully collecting and nurturing his plants. Be sure to take advantage of the Tea Room and, if time allows, some of the special classes. National Register of Historic Places. The garden is open daily 9am to 5pm during the growing season. The Center is open year-round.
97 Main St., South Paris, ME
(207) 743-8820
www.mclaughlingarden.org
mclgardn@megalink.net

• Butterfly Habitat Garden — Bridgton
This 2000 sq. ft. garden was designed by the Lakeside Garden Club and provides the perfect environment for the metamorphous of the butterfly. It was composed with scientific selection of shrubs, annuals, perennials and herbs. If you love butterflies, this is the place to come for inspiration.

Route 302, Bridgton, ME
(207) 647-3472
www.mainelakeschamber.com

Midcoast

• R.P. Coffin Wildflower Reservation — Woolwich
Considered one of the best wildflower collections in New England. Located in the rural and historic river-front community of Woolwich. Take Rt. 127 north out of Woolwich to merger with Rt. 128. Take Rt. 128 north and go about seven miles. You will pass the North Woolwich Methodist Church on your right. Go down and then up a steep hill and, at the top, take the road to the left at the Chop Point sign. There is a small parking area upon entry and the trail to the waterfront goes off to the right.
Chops Point Rd., Woolwich, ME

• Coastal Maine Botanical Garden — Boothbay
This is a relatively new endeavor begun in 1992. Woodland paths lead you through 128 acres and one mile of tidal shoreline. Some areas are planted. Long term plans include display gardens, native plant collections, library and visitor center. This may well warrant an annual visit if you wish to see how a large botanical garden evolves over time.
Barter's Island Rd., Boothbay, ME
(207) 633-4333
cmbg@clinic.net

• Christina's Garden at Olson House — Cushing
Maintained by the Farnsworth Museum in honor of the Wyeth family. If you are drawn by Andrew Wyeth's haunting painting of Christina's World, then you will definitely want to visit this quintessential Maine house and garden. The museum reestablished this small annual garden based on historic research. The site is known for its extremely old lilacs and roses.
Hawthorne Point Rd., Cushing, ME
(207) 354-0102
www.wyethcenter.com/olson/htm

• Camden Garden Theater — Camden
Elegant amphitheater designed by Fletcher Steele in 1929 and park designed by the Olmsted brothers during 1928-31. Fletcher Steele designed over 500 gardens, mostly private, concentrated in the eastern part of the country. He is most known for his work at Naumkeag in Stockbridge, Massachusetts; however, the

amphitheater is considered one of his finest works. Fredrick Law Olmsted was the founder of landscape architecture in this country. He and Calvert Vaux helped change the face of urban landscape with their design of Central Park in New York City. Olmsted's son and stepson greatly influenced public space in Maine, especially in the Camdem/Rockport area. The amphitheater offers scenic views over the harbor and is listed on the National Register of Historic Places.
Main St., Camden, ME
(207) 236-3440

• The Garden Institute at Merry Gardens — Camden
   This is a non-profit preserve offering educational and horticultural opportunities for the Midcoast area. Its attractions include a large herb garden, perennial gardens, test garden of annuals and abundant wildflowers, trees, shrubbery and a pond. A special attraction is the children's garden for those wishing to expose their children to the wonders of gardens and gardening.
Upper Mechanic St., Camden, ME
(207) 236-9064

• Merryspring Horticultural Nature Park — Camden
   This is a 66-acre park with gardens and trails through undeveloped fields and woods. There is a 10-acre arboretum of native species, woodland garden with a vernal pool and spectacular vistas of the surrounding mountains. The gazebo is surrounded by herb, rose, perennial gardens and raised beds.
Rt. 1, Conway Rd., Camden, ME
(207) 236-2239

• Johnny's Selected Seeds — Albion
   Here's something different for gardening lovers. Johnny's Selected Seeds is one of North America's largest vegetable and flower trial gardens and they allow you to visit their research and seed production farm. One-hour guided tours are conducted from June to September with self-guided tours also available. Group tours can also be arranged. The farm is closed to visitors on Sundays. Unfortunately, the retail store was closed mid-2001 so that the business could be focused on electronic commerce.
Foss Hill Rd., Albion, ME 04910
(207) 437-9294
heidi@johnnyseeds.com

Down East

• Colonel Black Mansion Formal Gardens — Ellsworth
   This is an 1842 house museum on 185 acres with community walking trails. The formal garden was laid out in 1903 and restored in the 1990s based on the original plans. National Register of Historic Places.
81 West Main St., Rt. 172, Ellsworth, ME
(207) 667-8671

• Beatrix Farrand Garden — College of the Atlantic, Bar Harbor
   This terraced garden was designed by Beatrix Farrand in 1928 and restored in 1990. Farrand was one of the most prominent landscape designers in America. Although she is most associated with Dumbarton Oaks in Washington, DC, she designed 40 gardens on Mt. Desert Island. Included among them is the Abby Aldrich Rockefeller Garden, considered to be one of the most beautiful in America. Be sure to stroll the entire College campus after viewing the garden.
Eden St., Rt. 3, Bar Harbor, ME
(207) 288-5015

• Asticou Azalea Garden — Northeast Harbor
   The state's finest Japanese-style garden, with more than 20 varieties of azaleas. Charles Savage, prominent landscape designer and Northeast Harbor resident, designed it in 1956 with numerous plants from Beatrix Farrand's private Bar Harbor home, Reef Point. Farrand established her garden with the intent that it be a center of study of native American plant life for a limited number of students. Fearing that it might become a tourist attraction, she dismantled the garden, providing plant resources for both the Asticou Azalea and Thuya Gardens.
Corner of Rts. 198 & 3, Northeast Harbor, ME
(207) 276-5130

• Thuya Gardens & Thuya Lodge — Northeast Harbor
   Charles Savage also designed these gardens in 1956 with long beds of perennials and annuals. There are outstanding specimen trees and also many shrubs from Beatrix Farrand's Reef Point collection. The lodge, a wonderful example of a Maine summer cottage, contains a botanical library.
Rt. 3 (Peabody Drive), Northeast Harbor, ME
(207) 276-5130

• Amen Farm Gardens — Brooklin
   Tree lovers should not miss this newly-planted arboretum featuring 150

uncommon trees.
Naskeag Point Rd., Brooklin, ME
(207) 359-8982

• Cottage Garden — Lubec
   This old-fashioned, two-acre cottage garden is just around the corner from Cobscook Bay. It features old-fashioned roses, delphiniums and the aroma of pinks.
North Lubec Rd., Lubec, ME
(207) 733-2902

Kennebec & Moose River Valleys

• Pine Tree State Arboretum — Augusta
   Established in 1981 on 224 acres. Collections include more than 300 trees and shrubs, a rock garden, rhododendrons, lilacs, plus one of the largest collections of hosta in New England. Trail system of 3.5 miles for hiking, jogging, skiing, snow-shoeing, mountain biking and horseback riding.
153 Hospital St., Augusta, ME
(207) 621-0031
www.communityforest.org

• Annie Sturgis Wildflower Sanctuary — Vassalboro
The sanctuary hosts 40 acres of mixed hardwoods and softwoods along the Kennebec River and Seven Mile Brook. Two miles of circular trails through large stands of bloodroot, Canada lily, dog's tooth, violets, trillium and pink lady's slippers. Look for the biggest stand of wild ginger in Maine. Maintained by the New England Wildflower Society.
Old Federal Rd., (west of, and parallel to, U.S. Rt. 201). Entrance opposite fire station in Riverside, Vassalboro, ME
(207) 621-0038

• Brewster Inn Gardens — Dexter
   Designed by noted Maine architect John Calvin Stevens in the 1930s. Stevens was commissioned by former Governor, State Representative and U.S. Senator Ralph Owen Brewster and his wife, Dorothy Foss, to convert Brewster's farmhouse to a mansion. At the same time Stevens and his associates created a landscape plan that included extensive formal gardens. The original stone retaining walls frame an acre of landscaped grounds containing a pergola, rose arbor and arched garden seats. Some plants from the original Stevens plan still remain. They

include Van Fleet roses, yews, clematis, hydrangea and a barberry hedge. The garden is now largely filled with informal plantings surrounded by stones purportedly collected by Mrs. Brewster on her world travels. The mansion, which is on the National Register of Historic Places, is currently a bed and breakfast and is open daily, year-round.
31 Zion's Hill, Dexter, ME
(207) 924-3130

Moosehead Lake & Katahdin

• Ecotat — Hermon
This 89-acre land trust celebrates the continuation of the life's work of Crosby family members, who lived here for 50 years. The trust contains developed gardens and trails with more than 140 species of trees and 1,500 perennials. A special library is available for both gardeners and birders.
Rt. 2 at crest of Miller Hill, Hermon, ME
(207) 848-3485

Annual Garden & Landscape Events

✦✦✦ *March — April* ✦✦✦

Greater Portland

Portland Flower Show
Four-day gala with exhibits, awards, lectures. Premier Maine horticultural event of the year and largest in New England.
(207) 775-4403
www.portlandgardenshow.com

Down East

Bangor Garden Show
Huge marketplace of gardening goods and Maine crafts. Weekend of family fun.
(207) 990-4444
www.bangorgardenshow.com

♦♦♦ *May* ♦♦♦

Western Mountains & Lakes

Lilac Festival
South Paris
(207) 743-8820

Maine Iris Society Show
South Paris
(207) 345-9532f

Down East

Warblers & Wildflowers Festival
Bar Harbor
(207) 288-5103

♦♦♦ *June* ♦♦♦

Southern Coastal

B&B Inn & Garden Tour
Arundel, Kennebunk, Kennebunkport
(207) 967-0857

Western Mountains & Lakes

Maine Iris Society Show
Auburn
(207) 782-2645

Midcoast

Hidden Treasures of the Boothbay Peninsula
Boothbay
Coastal Maine Botanical Garden, PO Box 234, Boothbay, ME 04537
(207) 633-4333
embg@clinic.net

Down East

Zonta Garden Tour
Bangor area
(207) 942-5117

Kennebec & Moose River Valleys

Summer Guided Tours (ongoing through August)
Pine Tree State Arboretum, Augusta
(207) 621-0031
www.communityforest.org

◆◆◆ *July* ◆◆◆

Western Mountains & Lakes

Lewiston-Auburn Annual Garden Tour
Lewiston-Auburn
(207) 782-1403

Midcoast

Miles Memorial Hospital League
House & Garden Tour
Damariscotta area
(207) 563-8791

Waldo County Hospital Aide
Garden Tour
Waldo County
(207) 338-3213

Camden-Rockport Garden Tour
Camden-Rockport
(207) 236-9797

Gemstones, Rocks & Gold

Gemstone in substrate, courtesy of Maine State Museum, Augusta

You might not immediately associate Maine with rock hounds and panning for gold; after all, we're known a lot more for our pine trees and lobsters. However, there is a lot of stone in Maine with a corresponding amount of crystals, semiprecious gems, gold and other minerals. The novice rock hound is virtually assured of finding something of interest at one of Maine's many collecting sites. And, for certain, the knowledgeable collector will find a treasure trove. Looking for gemstones or panning for gold may be rewarding in many ways. It's a very inexpensive and involving hobby that everyone can enjoy. At the same time it provides outdoor recreation and the opportunity to learn something about earth science. It's a wonderful opportunity to do something with the whole family, a group of your friends or just by yourself.

Many of Maine's best minerals are found in an igneous rock called pegmatite, a very coarse-grained granite. Pegmatites may contain beryl, topaz or Maine's famous state gemstone, the tourmaline. Tourmaline ranges in color from black or white to vibrant shades of red, green and blue. Individual crystals range from opaque to transparent and may be single or multi-colored. There is even a "watermelon" variety with a green outer layer surrounding a pink core. Tourmaline occurs as lustrous, elongated crystals that commonly have a rounded triangular cross section and narrow grooves running parallel to their long direction. The crystals range in size from microscopic to over a foot long. Transparent crystals may be clear enough to produce a faceted, cut gemstone. Others can be tumble-polished for use in various types of jewelry. Who knows, maybe you can turn one of your finds into a wonderful gift.

Warning:

You will typically find collection sites on private property. Obviously you should always get permission before entering private property. Getting permission for a given site might require a bit of ingenuity. To find out how, begin by asking the neighbors. The next step is to ask the locals at the nearest chamber of commerce or in the shops, restaurants or lodgings. If that doesn't work, call the local collecting club, checking the listings for key words like, rocks, minerals or gems. If you still need help, call one of the sources listed under "Equipment, Guides & Advice" found in this section. They probably can steer you to a local contact. We have not listed any site where we know general access is denied.

You can also find quite of bit of gold in Maine, too. Gold occurs in bedrock, in the sediments that the glaciers eroded from the bedrock and in stream deposits. Gold that is not concentrated in veins, but in unconsolidated sediments, is called "placer." Most of the gold found in Maine today comes from placer deposits in stream beds. Generally, gold panning activities in Maine do not require a permit as long as you adhere to the following restrictions.

1. The activity must be confined to sandy, gravelly or cobbled, non-vegetated streambeds with no disturbance of the stream banks.
2. The activity must be limited to the use of gold pans, sluices of less than 10 square feet or suction dredges with a hose diameter of four inches or less.
3. Permission must first be obtained from the landowner.

Much of northern and eastern Maine including the unorganized townships is under the jurisdiction of the Maine Land Use Regulation Commission (LURC). Regulations under this jurisdiction may be somewhat more restrictive than in the rest of Maine. A packet of information including a list of restricted stream segments and a map of lands under LURC jurisdiction can be obtained from:
Maine Land Use Regulation Commission
Department of Conservation`
22 State House Station
Augusta, ME 04333-0022
Tel: (207) 287-2631 or (800) 452-8711
www.state.me.us/doc/lurc/lurchome.htm

Listed below you will find sites for rockhounding and panning for gold, mineral exhibits and sources for equipment, guides and advice. Happy prospecting.

Southern Coastal

Rock Hound Sites

• Dundee Falls — Near Windham
Look for black tourmaline — what a special gift you could make out of a find like that. Also keep your eye out for beryl, (green, white and blue varieties) and a host of other minerals. Go north from the intersection of the River Road and Rt. 202 in Windham. Continue past Gambo Road on left. Look for road with a gate on right across from large white farmhouse with attached barn. Park and walk the road to the dam.

• The Den — Near Gorham
This is the site to bring the whole family to and make it an adventure. Look for small gem red garnets (in the streambed) and large garnets in the stream cut ledges. Follow Rt. 237 north from the intersection of Rt. 237 and Rt. 25 in Gorham. Go straight across Rt. 202 for .75 miles. Turn right onto Gambo Rd. (across from Dunlap Rd.) Follow Gambo to the dam where the road ends. There is a large parking area.

Western Mountains & Lakes

Rock Hound Sites

• Black Mountain — Near Rumford
You could be very fortunate here by keeping your eye out for pink tourmaline. Also check for beryl and apatite. From the junction of Rt. 2 with Rt. 120 in Rumford, go north on Rt. 120 for 8.1 miles. Turn left after a small construction company. Follow Black Mountain Rd. (dirt) for 2.2 miles to another dirt road on your left. Follow the road to the first split. The road on the right goes to the Black Mountain Mine.

• Tower Area — Near Rumford
Look for beryl and blue tourmaline in blasted rock. See immediately preceding directions. On Black Mountain Rd. take the dirt road that splits to the left.

• The Bemis Stream Prospect — Near Mexico

You may well find tourmalines of various colors. There's a good chance of finding apatite too. From the junction of Rt. 2 and Rt. 17 in the town of Mexico, go north 17.1 miles on Rt. 17 to the Houghton settlement area. Turn left on a road in the middle of a field. You will see a small bridge and a sign saying "Houghton." Go 6.3 miles to the bridge crossing the Bemis Stream and park just after the bridge. Walk to the steep ledge and look there and across from it where the blast rock went.

• Pitts & Tenney Mine — Near Minot

This is a famous garnet location, known for its fine orange garnets that measure up to five inches across. Imagine bringing something like that home. Follow Rts. 121 & 11 from Auburn to Minot, turning right onto Rt. 119 north. Go about one mile and you will see a large ranch house set back into a ledge. After you pass the house, a road will be on your left. Follow this mine road up the hill, bearing to the left.

• Tamminen & Waisanen Mines — Near Norway

A miner by the name of Nestor Tamminen worked his namesake site by hand for many years. He dumped a great deal of tourmaline-laden rock as he mined for feldspar. You just might find a treasure in his old dumps. One collector took out a football-shaped and sized quartz crystal and another got a three-inch diameter green tourmaline crystal that was six inches long. The Waisanen is the first pit you will come to when you enter the area. The minerals are the same kind found at the Tamminen, as it is the same pegmatite. From the intersection of Rts. 118 & 117 in Norway, go west on Rt. 118 for about one mile. Turn right onto Greenwood Rd. Go 5.3 miles to the Richardson Hollow Rd. Go about one half mile to the parking area. The path in front of the parking area leads to the Mamminen and Waisanen Mines.

Gold Panning — Known Sources

• Swift River and Its Tributaries — Byron Area
These are located in both Oxford and Franklin Counties. In DeLorme's Maine Atlas & Gazetteer see Map 18, C-5.

• Sandy River — Madrid to New Sharon
This source is located in Franklin County. In DeLorme's Maine Atlas & Gazetteer see Maps 19, A-2 and 20, D-2.

• Gold Brook — Chain of Ponds Township & Kibby Township
This aptly named brook is found in Franklin County. In DeLorme's Maine Atlas & Gazetteer see Map 28, A-5 and Map 39, D-2.

• Gold Brook — Chase Stream Township
The golden name continues. This brook is located Somerset County. In DeLorme's Maine Atlas & Gazetteer see Map 40, C-4.

• Gold Brook — Appleton Township
The golden name continues through Somerset County. In DeLorme's Maine Atlas & Gazetteer see Map 39, D-2.

• Nile Brook — Dallas Plantation; Rangely
This source flows through Franklin County. In DeLorme's Maine Atlas & Gazetteer see Map 29, E-1 and 28 E-5.

• St. Croix River — Woodland (Baileyville)
This Canadian border river flows along Washington County. In DeLorme's Atlas & Gazetteer see Map 36, C-4.

Alert: Topographic maps covering these areas can be purchased from local sporting goods stores and bookstores. These may also be purchased from the Maine Geological Survey, State House Station #22, Augusta, ME 04333. Tel: (207) 287-2801

Equipment, Guides & Advice

• Larry Bilodeau — Lewiston
   Larry can be reached at 27 Gina St., Lewiston, ME 04240 or by telephone (207) 784-0302.

• Perham's — West Paris
   This combination store and private mineral museum is located at Rt. 1 (junction of Rts. 26 & 219), West Paris, ME 04289. Telephone is (207) 674-2341. The museum is open during store hours, seven days a week, 9am to 5pm.

• Rosey and Jerry Perrier — Byron
   Rosey and Jerry can be reached at HC 62, Box 48, Byron, ME 04275 or by telephone (207) 364-3880

• Winthrop Mineral Shop — East Winthrop
   This shop is located on Rt. 202, East Winthrop, ME 04343. Telephone is (207) 395-4488.

Something Special

• Poland Mining Camps — Poland
   If you are a serious rock hound and want a place to stay that caters to rock and mineral collectors, you have found it at the Poland Mining Camps. Everything (lodging, meals, mine fees and guide) is included in one price. Cost is based on choice of lodging and length of stay. Reservations are required and the season runs from Memorial Day to September 30. It is located on Rt. 26 in Poland just before the junction with Rt. 11. Dudy and Mary Groves have exclusive collecting access to several mines.
   PO Box 26, Poland, ME 04274
   Tel: (207) 998-2350
   www.polandminingcamps.com

Midcoast

Rock Hound Sites

• Standpipe Hill — Near Topsham
   This place has the reputation for the finest gem blue beryl in the world! Take Winter St. out from the intersection of Rts. 24 & 201 in the center of Topsham Village. Take dead end Abenaki Drive to end and park. Take the trail into the woods. Take a right turn at the intersection and head toward the tower and the Standpipe location. If you continue to the second intersection and turn right you will reach other mines that have beryl and other minerals of interest.

• Porcupine Hill — Near Topsham
   This is where you might find a very fine black tourmaline as well as quartz crystals, apatites and garnets. From Topsham go north on Rt. 196. After you past I-95 you will see the Topsham Mobile Home Park. Turn into the park on Andrea St. and go to the end and park by the brick building. There you will find a trail to the quartz crystal pits.

• Coombs Mine — Near Bowdoinham
   This is supposed to be one the "forgotten great mines" that no one pays much attention to. Too bad, because in the ledges and pits you can find green and gold

beryl, amethyst, aqua and garnets. Get off I-295 at the Bowdoinham exit. Follow Rt. 138 west to Rt. 201 to Rt. 125. Turn right on Rt. 125 and go .75 miles. There you will see a driveway with a stone wall beside the road. The driveway is the mine road and you should park elsewhere and/or seek permission to use it. The mine is about one half mile in.

Down East

Rock Hound Sites

• Jasper Beach — Machiasport

This is a long, stone beach named for the jasper stone. Real jasper is hard to come by in Maine — a few pieces can be found in glacial gravel near the Quebec border in far western Maine. True jasper is a form of silica that is enriched in iron. Unfortunately, this beach "jasper" is actually a fine-grained, reddish-brown volcanic rock called rhyolite. It doesn't quite have the bright red color of real jasper. However, it is attractive due to the polished surface formed by constant abrasion against sand grains. Happily, collecting is allowed and the "jasper" will make a nice keepsake. Take Machias Rd. south from Machiasport. The beach is just south of Bucks Harbor.

For additional reading related to Gemstones, Rocks & Gold we would like to recommend the following books.

• A Field Guide to Rocks and Minerals, F. H. Pough, 1976, Houghton Mifflin, Boston, 317 pages

• Maine Mining Adventures, C. J. Stevens, 1994, John Wade, Publisher, PO Box 303, Phillips, ME 04966, 208 pages

• The Next Bend in the River (Gold Mining in Maine), C. J. Stevens, 1989, John Wade, Publisher, PO Box 303, Phillips, ME 04966, 177 pages

• Guidebook 1 to Mineral Collecting in the Maine Pegmatite Belt, Federation of Maine Mineral and Gem Clubs, 1983, privately published and sold by mineral shops; provides directions to collecting sites, 22 pages

• Maine's Treasure Chest — Gems and Minerals of Oxford County, J. C. Perham, 1987, Perham's Mineral Store, West Paris, ME, describes most of the popular collecting sites and their histories, 260 pages

Giving — The Maine Way

The AltMaine Guide can only give you a small sampling of how wonderful this State of Maine truly is. As you travel it, enjoy its beauty and meet its people you can gain a much deeper sense of this special place. Hopefully you have a sense that very little of what we have today "just happened." If fact, if you read through the short biographies in the Great Contributors to Maine section, you will begin to get a sense that a great deal of contributing, by a large number of people, has made Maine the unique and engaging place it is.

You may be a native Mainer, a summer resident or someone with the opportunity to spend only a few weeks or days here. But if you feel like you would like to contribute to Maine, we would like to take you now to where no other guidebook does. We encourage you to contribute to one (or more) of the three causes we describe in this section. We believe that these three very much help keep Maine the Maine we want to protect. Obviously there are many other good Maine causes and we hope in editions to come that they too will be featured. These three deal with various walks of Maine life. One is concerned with protecting our food and soils and nurturing our small-scale agrarian lifestyle. Another is concerned with raising the quality of information, education and entertainment that comes to us over the airwaves. Still another creates programs that build on community assets and resources to strengthen those communities over time. We trust you will enjoy reading about their missions and accomplishments.

And, thank you for Giving — The Maine Way!

Maine Organic Farmers and Gardeners Association

The Mission of the Maine Organic Farmers and Gardeners Association is to:

• Help farmers and gardeners grow organic food
• Protect the environment
• Promote stewardship of natural resources
• Increase local food production
• Support sustainable rural communities
• Illuminate the connections among healthy food, environmentally-sound farming practices and vital local communities

MOFGA was founded in 1971 and has grown from a loose affiliation of farmers and gardeners committed to growing healthy, chemical-free food to an internationally-recognized advocate for local, organic food production that protects the ecological, economic and social viability of Maine's rural communities. Today MOFGA is one of the oldest and largest organic organizations in the country with over 3,500 individual, family and business members.

The Common Ground Country Fair

MOFGA sponsors this celebration that draws nearly 50,000 visitors each September to Unity, Maine. The fair is a wonderful celebration of sustainable rural living for all. Fairgoers can visit farmers and their livestock, eat delicious, Maine-grown organic foods, enjoy music, learn basic gardening skills, see vendors of Maine-made crafts, folk arts, foods, plants, agricultural tools and environmentally-friendly products. Over 1,200 volunteers make the event happen!

Year-round Education

Unity, Maine, is the home for MOFGA all year round. Workshops on subjects ranging from organic apple production to low-impact forestry, from cheesemaking to marketing farm products, are offered throughout the year, along with sessions on the road. Schedules are available at the MOFGA website, www.mofga.org, and in the quarterly MOFGA newspaper, distributed to members and sold on newsstands across the State.

A Few Other MOFGA Activities

The organization also manages a "MOFGA CERTIFIED ORGANIC" program, provides technical assistance to farmers and gardeners in Maine and throughout the nation, promotes creative approaches to pesticide reduction and proposes bills dealing with subjects such as genetic cross contamination. MOFGA also offers Apprenticeship and Journeyperson Programs to help develop and sustain farming skills among new farmers.

If you are interested in any of MOFGA's activities, we encourage you to contact:

MOFGA, PO Box 170, Unity, Maine 04988
Tel: (207) 568-4142 or check the MOFGA website at www.mofga.org for events, contacts and membership information.

maine public broadcasting

The mission of Maine Public Broadcasting is to engage the minds and enrich the lives of people in Maine and beyond with programs that inform, educate, entertain and inspire.

Public broadcasting in Maine recently celebrated its 40th anniversary and Maine Public Broadcasting's services have grown to national recognition. Maine PBS has one of the highest member-to-viewer ratios in the country with more than 40,000 annual contributors. Recently it became Maine's first digital television broadcaster. Maine Public Radio has been awarded Station of the Year honors from the AP for five years in a row, while its 22,000-plus membership ranks as one of the nation's largest member-supported public radio stations.

Television programs designed to better serve the people of Maine include public affairs coverage of local issues on Maine PBS. With the Governor as a regular guest, "Capitol Connection," a "live," call-in program, connects Maine's decision-makers with Maine's citizens. "Maine Watch," in its 16th season, brings together public officials, activists and community leaders to participate in a weekly issues and debate program.

Maine Public Radio continues to bring its listeners locally-produced classical music programming, statewide speaking events on "Speaking in Maine," National Public Radio programming along with local news three times a day. Listeners are kept abreast of current events with the award-winning "Morning Edition," "Midday" and "Maine Things Considered" programs.

All of Maine PBS' offerings emphasize education. "Teaching with ME" profiles the state's Teacher of the Year nominees from York to Presque Isle. Maine PBS also trains master teachers in the art of technology as part of a National Teacher Training Institute project. More than 100 teachers received educational enrichment throughout the state. While producing mini-documentaries during the second season of "Youth Voices," Maine PBS worked with 12 community youth groups, statewide substance abuse offices and provided online forums and websites.

The support shown for Maine Public Broadcasting, the state's largest member-based organization, is a testament to community spirit. Maine Public

Broadcasting continues to grow as a valued and trusted service. With the addition of streaming capabilities on the Internet at www.mpbc.org, Maine PBS and Maine Public Radio are now reaching an international audience.

Your Support Makes Quality Non-Commercial Programming Possible!
Mailing Address:
Membership, Maine Public Broadcasting
65 Texas Avenue
Bangor, Maine 04401

Volunteer: 1-800-884-1717
Visit on-line: www.mpbc.org

MAINE COMMUNITY FOUNDATION
Fulfilling the promise of giving

The Maine Community Foundation (MCF) is the leading charitable resource for donors seeking to provide long-term support to strengthen Maine communities.

MCF was founded in 1983 and is one of the largest foundations in Maine. It is an invested pool of permanent, charitable funds, the income from which benefits Maine's non-profit organizations and students. Each fund carries out the charitable purpose specified by the individual donor. People of varying economic means can become philanthropists by investing in the Foundation. MCF currently holds approximately 600 donor funds.

The Foundation is also a source of information, inspiration and networking. Grantmaking is focused on programs and projects that build on the assets and resources of Maine communities, with a special emphasis on sustainability.

Some of MCF's top contributions to Maine include:

• Providing funds to seed great ideas and organizations, including Kids Count, Maine Children's Alliance, Maine Philanthropy Center, Mainely Girls, The Game Loft, CyberSeniors.com, Life Jackets, Maine Children's Museum, Portland Trails and the Maine Chapter of Habitat for Humanity.

• Expanding philanthropy in Maine. Common Good, Maine Initiatives, Maine Women's Fund and some United Ways started as funds at the Foundation.

• Directing significant financial resources to rural parts of the state. A network of nearly 100 local and regional advisors helps to raise and allocate philanthropic resources for their own communities.

• Leveraging over $15 million in financial support for Maine from national foundations, including the Ford Foundation, Betterment Fund and the Wallace-Reader's Digest Foundation.

Innovative thinking and a statewide knowledge of Maine communities characterize MCF's grant program. Scholarships help support public policy research, classical voice training and studies in journalism. Current grants also fund conservation easements, support mentoring programs, help preserve historic treasures, underwrite environmental literature and even provide awards to students who demonstrate "the qualities of joy, dedication, self-discipline and fair play...."

If you would like to help support communities in Maine, please contact Carl Little at the Maine Community Foundation:

**(877) 700-6800 toll-free or
via email at clittle@mainecf.org**

Great Contributors to Maine

A great deal of The AltMaine Guide is centered on wonderful places to visit and interesting and enjoyable things to do. However, the essence of Maine is its people. The people of Maine are very much like people elsewhere. We may be somewhat more highly attuned to our environment though, whether we live along the coast, in rural farmlands, in the Great North Woods, along our rivers and lakes, among our mountains or in our cities. And Mainers are natural givers. The culture of giving and sharing runs deep in Maine and is, perhaps, an outcome of our early history when survival in a difficult and sometimes hostile environment depended upon community giving. Newcomers to Maine are quickly attracted to our culture of giving and it is not uncommon to see them rapidly become givers in the political, religious, economic, cultural, educational and environmental realms.

This section is intended to honor 10 exceptional contributors to the state of Maine. Picking 10 among a very large number of Great Contributor candidates was not easy, and in subsequent editions we hope to honor many more deserving individuals. We did try to balance our selections on the basis of type of contribution and, to a certain extent, their location throughout the state. In the confines of a few paragraphs we can only hint at what they have given. However, in honoring them in this small way, we also hope to encourage our readers to become greater contributors in their own right. We can all flourish when our citizens contribute meaningfully of time, talent and treasure. Hopefully you will enjoy learning how these ten became Great Contributors to Maine.

Clinton B. "Bill" Townsend

Clean air, clear water and free-flowing rivers filled with abundant fish life are synonymous with Maine. But that wasn't inevitable and, in fact, may not have been the case were it not for a very few people like Bill Townsend.

Bill moved to Canaan, Maine, with his wife Louise back in 1957, replacing an "impersonal and abstract corporate law practice" that he left behind in Connecticut with "the real problems of real people in Central Maine." In 1958 he became a director of the Somerset County Soil and Water Conservation District and in 1960, he became a director of the Natural Resources Council of Maine. NRCM was then just a council of environmental organizations functioning without a staff. Bill became NRCM President in 1965 (serving through 1970) and began a lifelong commitment to three issues: water pollution, the indiscriminate use of pesticides and river protection.

In the 1960s, Maine's major rivers were open sewers, filled with untreated industrial and human waste. Raw chicken parts were dumped into Belfast Harbor and fish kills took place every summer across the state. Fumes from the rivers peeled paint off houses and, in Augusta, the State House windows were often closed in summer due to the stench emanating from the Kennebec River. DDT was sprayed on Maine's forests to kill spruce budworm and other insects without consideration for the horrific side effects on fish and wildlife. Dam proposals by the Army Corps of Engineers and private organizations would have flooded out both the St. John and Allagash Rivers. Additionally, nuclear power plants and oil refineries on the coast, rampant development, acid rain and assaults on The Great North Woods required the attention of Bill and the NRCM over the last 40 years.

In 1973 Bill became Chairman of the Maine Chapter of The Nature Conservancy where he subsequently created a full-time professional staff. He served two years as President and another four on the Board. In 1986 he became a director of the Atlantic Salmon Federation (ASF) and has remained a director since that time. As one of three Presidentially-appointed Commissioners to the North Atlantic Salmon Conservation Organization, he helped bring the Greenland marine fishery for Atlantic salmon into its present science-based mode. And during the 1980s and 90s he was deeply involved through NRCM and ASF to defeat unwise dam proposals including the Big A on the upper Penobscot, the Bangor Dam, The Basin Mills Dam on the main-stem Penobscot and the Edwards Dam on the Kennebec.

Bill says that when he first began addressing environmental issues 40 years ago, there was practically no legal and regulatory framework at either state or federal level to address the problems. Today, thanks to Bill and a few other dedicated people, a strong framework does exist. He thinks, however, that in a sense we are victims of our success, that issues are now much more subtle and complex, requiring scientists, lawyers and managers to navigate in a much more complicated governmental arena.

As he looks into the future, Bill sees enormous challenges ahead. Toxins must be contained and pollution prevented; the rivers need to flow freely and support fish life; the water must remain clear and the air clean. We all need to work together to make this happen, but it's nice to know a committed and highly knowledgeable Bill Townsend will be out front, leading.

Duane D. "Buzz" Fitzgerald

The success of Maine or, for that matter, any state is premised on a healthy economy where a large majority can be meaningfully employed. Buzz Fitzgerald not only ensured that large numbers of Mainers were meaningfully employed, but also that they had a stake in shaping their economic futures.

Buzz is a native of St. John Plantation, on the St. John River in far northern Maine. In his words, he was born in a house "served by neither indoor plumbing nor electricity." His father had no education beyond the first year of high school and worked in the woods in the winter and as a guide on the Allagash River in summer. In 1940, Buzz's father secured a helper's job at the Bath Iron Works (BIW) and a special chemistry was born that took the father to head of all the steel trades and the son to President and CEO some 52 years later.

Buzz graduated from Morse High School in Bath, then went on to Boston University where he received degrees from the College of General Studies, School of

Management and School of Law. He returned to Bath and, for 23 years, practiced law and served as outside counsel to BIW. He joined BIW as Executive Vice President in 1986 and, in 1991, he assumed leadership of Maine's largest private employer and one of the country's major shipbuilders.

Life was not easy in his new role and he inherited a company racked by discord following a bitter strike in 1985. Buzz was committed to repairing relationships within his organization and recruited several courageous union leaders to help craft a unique labor agreement. That agreement provided for shared decision-making and pioneered "interest-based bargaining." Instead of separate meetings, offers and counter offers, both sides met together to create a joint agreement. This approach helped dispel decades of antipathy between those who build ships and those who oversee their work. Buzz's pioneering agreement became a national model and on Labor Day, 1994, President Bill Clinton came to BIW to help celebrate his successful approach to labor relations.

The consensus-building skills that Buzz acquired have been put to good use. He has served on the Boards of United Airlines, Blue Cross and Blue Shield of Maine and the Central Maine Power Group and was appointed the First Chairman of The Maine Jobs Council. He also served as a Trustee of Boston University and the University of Maine System and as a Fellow of The American College of Trial Lawyers. He is recipient of many awards including the Edmund S. Muskie Access to Justice Award.

In recent years Buzz has put his consensus-building skills to work in the areas of gay and lesbian rights and handgun control, serving as Honorary Co-Chair of Maine Citizens Against Handgun Violence.

Today the man, whom Governor King called "a wise man" and the person to call at midnight or 6 am when an intractable problem was in dire need of ethical guidance, fights the twin assaults of lung and brain cancer. Nevertheless, he uses this time to offer counsel to fellow cancer sufferers and encourages them to keep going and reminds them that "Time is precious. Don't squander it."

The man who made consensus building a hallmark of his career is today himself the subject of consensus among all that know him; *this is one fine person and a great contributor!*

Elinor "Ellie" Goldberg

Most people would join Ellie Goldberg in saying that nothing is more important than the children of Maine. What distinguishes Ellie is that her life is largely devoted to improving the lot of Maine's children.

This engaging and energetic lady is the founding Executive Director of the Maine Children's Alliance (MCA), which began in 1994 with only herself as staff. Without help and a limited budget she began to create a viable, multi-issue child-advocacy organization that could provide critical information about children. Information that in turn could be used to support political action campaigns, provide advocacy for legislation and support efforts for systemic reform in the delivery of governmental services for children. Her mission statement reads, "...to be a strong and powerful voice to improve the lives of all Maine's children, youth, and families."

Ellie knew that collaboration was the key to success and both founded and worked with several collaborative projects. In 1998 she helped create the Start ME Right coalition, composed of children's advocates and legislators. They sought funding increases for early childhood care and education. This resulted in an additional $15 million for new and increased services for young Maine children and their parents. Start ME Right is an ongoing initiative, directing efforts to 65,000 Maine children who are cared for out of the home every day, and 33,000 Maine children whose parents need financial support for child care costs.

Another of Ellie's key initiatives is School Based Health Services. MCA works in support of the (currently 20) School Based Health Centers (SBHCs) where the children are, and where there is a unique capacity to attend to their needs. Providing physical and mental health services to school-aged children helps them remain in school and ready to learn. Ancillary benefits include reduction of parental work absences, helping keep children out of Emergency Rooms and detecting illness and risk early to avoid later, more expensive treatment. Statistics from SBHCs provide ample evidence of the need for such centers and for expanded services. Of all diagnoses, over a third were for mental health issues, yet 50 percent of the SBHCs currently provide no mental health services to students. This is an area Ellie is particularly addressing, bringing providers, insurers, researchers and school personnel together to build an expanded mental health services component. In time, this initiative will provide information to schools and communities that will enable them to access available funding for screening and services and to better protect our student children.

In only six years Ellie has grown MCA from a staff of one to six and a budget from $50,000 to $390,000. She has done a great deal of good and realizes a great deal more needs to be done. On the MCA website there is a section devoted to "Actions for Kids By Kids." It provides a list of "speak out actions" that kids can take to improve their situations in their family, neighborhood and community, school and in "The Bigger Picture." It ends with this quote: "It isn't easy being a kid...these actions won't necessarily make it easier, but they can't hurt — in fact they usually do make things better...you can make a change...."

Certainly Ellie has made a change — a great change for the better.

Evan D. Richert

The State of Maine not only has accomplished, but will continue to accomplish a great deal of good — largely due to its astute planning. And, when you think of planning in the State of Maine, you're likely to think of the Director of the Maine State Planning Office, Evan Richert.

It's not surprising that this thoughtful man became the Director of the Maine State Planning Office because planning is evident throughout his life. On the academic front he received a Master of Regional Planning degree from Syracuse University and today is an adjunct professor in the Muskie School at the University of Southern Maine, where he teaches community development and planning. He is also a member of the American Institute of Certified Planners and the Growing Smart Directorate of the American Planning Association — an organization chartered to rewrite state model legislation to govern state and local planning.

Most of Evan's work, however, has been outside the academic environment and he has had plenty of experience on "the front lines." He served as Planner, Greater Portland Council of Governments from 1975-77 and as Planning Director for the City of South Portland from 1977-81. He also knows planning from the commercial side and, from 1981-95, was President of Market Decisions, Inc., in South Portland. Along with other co-owners, Evan grew a two-person consulting firm into a 20-person full-service market research and community planning company with public and private clients throughout the Northeast.

Evan's background serves him (and Maine) well today in his current role. He directs the 60-person State Planning Office — the policy and planning arm of state government in the areas of natural resources, community planning, economy, energy and governmental affairs. He is an ex-officio member of the Cabinet and is currently Chair of the Land and Water Resources Council and Land for Maine's Future. He has also served as Commissioner of the Maine Indian Tribal-State Commission and Board Member of the Maine Development Foundation.

Evan is highly cognizant of the fact that Maine, relative to other states, has an abundance of natural wealth, but far less economic wealth. He cites the traditional public policy debate which often translates to "pickerel vs. payroll," "national park vs. industrial forest," "Atlantic salmon vs. hydropower and aquaculture," and "wildlife habitat vs. suburban sprawl."

But Evan is thinking (and planning) beyond this to a stage where we approach issues in a different way...a way that "needn't compromise either our natural treasure or the quest for economic wellbeing." He calls this "the next industrial revolution," and it is characterized not by using up natural advantages to create wealth, but by maintaining and even enhancing the natural treasure. Evan says that "the next industrial revolution" is already underway in Maine, combining knowledge-based economic initiatives with a vibrant ecology. He believes that we are "well positioned" for it, but "we have a heck of a lot of work to get there."

What Evan didn't say is that well before the work, there will be a lot of planning. And aren't we fortunate to have someone in charge who loves planning...and loves Maine.

Kenneth "Ken" Curtis

Ken Curtis was born and raised in Curtis Corner, Leeds, Maine. It was, at the time, a pretty bleak rural setting. Educational opportunities consisted of a small, one-room school serving all eight grades and a junior high school that attracted three students. Job opportunities for young people were few, low paying and requiring minimal skills. The existing housing was largely sub-standard and the political environment was mired in mediocrity, maintaining the status quo. Ken Curtis became disenchanted and resolved to do something about it.

After high school Ken went to the Maine Maritime Academy in Castine, served in the Merchant Marine and saw active duty in the U.S. Navy as a Lieutenant Commander during the Korean Conflict. He then went on to graduate from the Portland University Law. Ken assumed a series of responsibilities, ever increasing his knowledge and scope. He served first as Assistant to Congressman James Oliver, then worked at the Legal Division of the U.S. Library of Congress, and then became Field

Coordinator for the Area Redevelopment Administration for Maine with the U.S. Department of Commerce. In 1965 he became Secretary of State of Maine and in 1967 was elected Maine's Governor. The status quo was about to change.

During the eight years (1967-1975) Ken served Maine as a Democratic Governor, the Legislature was heavily Republican. What he was able to achieve was accomplished only through excellent human relations skills and the joint action of the Executive and Legislative branches. During Ken's Administration Maine's Government became modernized. Two hundred departments, bureaus and boards were reorganized into 15 principal commissions that form the Governor's Cabinet as we know it today. Critical new departments and agencies were added, including the State Planning Office, Department of Environmental Protection, the Land Use Regulation Commission, the Maine Housing Authority and the Human Rights Commission.

Ken's administration enacted key legislation including the State District Attorney System, Shore Land Zoning, Minimum Lot Size Law, Oil Conveyance Law, Site Selection Law, Saco River Corridor and Commission, State Employees Labor Relations Act and The Allagash Wilderness Waterway. His administration also addressed the State's huge financial problem, enacting The Personal and Corporate Income Tax. This law was highly controversial, but Ken and his administration saw it as the least regressive way to raise needed funds. The wisdom of his approach was evident in the subsequent repeal referendum that failed overwhelmingly.

Other milestones include the creation of 25 regional vocational schools, appointment of the first female judge, the first Franco-American Chief Justice of the Superior Court and the First Native American Indian Commissioner.

Ken has eleven honorary degrees and has served on various corporate, educational and non-profit boards. Perhaps none is more important than his role on the Board of Trustees for the Susan L. Curtis Foundation. It oversees and funds Camp Susan Curtis, named for Ken's daughter, who died of Cystic Fibrosis. Unlike many Maine camps that are the enclave of affluent children from other states, Camp Susan Curtis provides the summer camp experience for deserving, but non-affluent Maine kids.

Sometimes you may find yourself wondering about the status quo and whether or not you can change it. You should know you can. Just ask Ken Curtis.

Lucy Poulin

For most of us, home is where the heart is. But, for Lucy Poulin, h.o.m.e. is where her heart is, and has been, for a long time. h.o.m.e. is an acronym that now stands on its own, but originally stood for Homeworkers Organized for More Employment. Lucy, a former Carmelite nun, founded this economic cooperative for the poor and elderly in an old farmhouse on Rt. 1 in Orland, back in 1970.

Lucy knew full well how society treated the least advantaged, having grown up poor on a Maine farm and having worked in a chicken plant. She began helping by providing additional income to the poor and elderly through the sale of their handcrafts, particularly quilts. Lucy, whom many still call Sister Lucy, also realized that the economic needs of Hancock County's rural poor could not be met solely with craft sales. She, and those who helped her start h.o.m.e., began to recognize and deal with the underlying causes of local poverty; lack of education, jobs, and social services, rising land costs, the decline of farming, the isolation of families, transportation problems and the long Maine winters. And then things really began to happen.

Lucy and her associates started programs to provide crafts training, basic education, child daycare, farm assistance, outreach services and housing. They encouraged hope and self-respect with a practical, "waste nothing," Yankee approach. Their approach has worked and those who have been helped have come back by the hundreds to volunteer their own help.

h.o.m.e. Inc. today is a village — a village dedicated to helping. Among the buildings you will find:

• A Craft Store that carries products made at h.o.m.e. as well as consignment items from hundreds of Maine crafters

• A Learning Center that offers free adult education and pre-GED classes while providing daycare for low-income families

• A Recovery & Bargain Barn where many are helped with donated clothing, furniture, appliances, toys, records, books, etc.

• A Market Stand & Food Bank housing a soup kitchen, shelves stocked to help feed many needy and a place to buy snacks, soda and juice and various necessities.

• A Garage where h.o.m.e. mechanics keep the motor pool's donated vehicles running and do auto repair at reasonable rates

• A Volunteer Center where volunteers have a place to stay with bunkrooms, kitchenette and showers available

• A Shingle Mill, Saw Mill, Woodworking Shops, Pottery Studio, Weaving Studio and Greenhouse to build houses, create jobs and make and grow things for sale

• A Chapel for worship and meetings.

Sister Lucy and her associates believe in four principles: help those in need, help people help themselves, help communities, not just individuals, and overcome oppression. She also welcomes contributions to h.o.m.e., Inc. at PO Box 10, Orland, ME 04472 and encourages requests for craft catalogs, volunteer help and donations.

If you do contribute in some small way, you can contribute to the four principles — and Maine — just like Sister Lucy does.

Marion Fuller Brown

When you drive through Maine you will, of course, be struck by its great beauty. Not so obvious is what you don't see and what contributes so much to the beauty. In Maine you are hard pressed to find a billboard, and that is largely due to the efforts of the unsinkable (and much beloved) Marion Fuller Brown.

In 1966 Marion was elected to the Maine Legislature, serving three terms from 1966 to 1972. She was quickly appointed to the Natural Resources Committee that was involved in the passage of many of our far-reaching environmental laws including the Clean Water and Clean Air legislation. As a legislator it was her sense that the traveling public didn't come to Maine to see billboards and assessed that they were largely the preserve of national advertisers for products like liquor and cigarettes — providing little if any advantage to local Maine businesses. In 1969 she sponsored the Maine Highway Beautification Bill calling for the removal of all billboards. The bill incurred the wrath of the powerful billboard lobby and only through her conviction, great tenacity and three trips to the State Supreme Court did the bill become law in 1977. Marion oversaw the completion of her initiative with the removal of the last billboard in 1981.

Marion's political efforts in Maine inevitably led to a national forum and she subsequently served as Republican National Committee Woman (1966-72), delegate to the National Republican Conventions (1964, 1968, 1972), appointed member of the National Highway Beautification Commission (1971-75). She was then founder (1978) and later president (1980) of Scenic America in Washington, D.C. She was also a member of the first Delegation of Friendship Among Women on a trip to the Peoples Republic of China in 1975. Marion also served the Garden Club of America in a host of roles, most notably as Vice Chairman of the Executive Committee (1986-88).

It's back in Maine, however, where Marion continues to make her unending contributions to our quality of life. At the local level she works to keep what she calls our "community values" and serves on the Board of Directors of the Old York Historical Society. There her mission is to save the historical facades that she deems as important as saving the natural environment. She believes that the "built environment" helps us to "keep the community values" that she treasures. She still serves on the Board of the York Land Trust, which she helped found in 1986. Her current passion is the Mt. Agamenticus Challenge — seeking to fund preservation of 7000 acres of land officially designated by The Nature Conservancy as "One of 200 Last Great Places in Amercia."

At the state level Marion also continues to serve on the Maine Travel Advisory Council, having been appointed by no less than four governors. Her contributions to the state of Maine have been such that Governor Angus King chose to recognize them on the occasion of her 80th birthday. His Proclamation read, "Now, therefore, I, Angus S. King, Jr., Governor of the State of Maine, do hereby proclaim May 14, 1997, as Marion Fuller Brown Day throughout the State of Maine, and urge all citizens to recognize her outstanding commitment and dedication to serving the people of Maine."

Marion says she is happiest in the country — that when she looks out the window of her Maine home to the fields and river beyond, "it's a tonic for my soul." As we travel the highways and byways of Maine we experience the contributions of Marion Fuller Brown, and it's a tonic for our souls, too.

Mort Mather

A good part of the life of Maine is devoted to small-scale farming, healthy living, concern for the environment and creating a meaningful cultural life with a small population spread over a large area. This would be a good description of Mort Mather too — if you threw in an offbeat and self-deprecating sense of humor.

Mort first came to Maine as stage manager for the Ogunquit Playhouse in the summer of 1966. In 1969 he married Barbara Jones, whom he had met at the Playhouse, and they purchased a house and farm. A couple of years later they left New York City for good and unknowingly became part of the back-to-the-land movement. In Mort's words, "I bought the farm because the sun set out across the field in back. At $16,000 I figured if the house rotted into the cellar hole the day after I bought it, I'd still be ahead."

Barbara dragged Mort away from a Monday Night football game to the first meeting of the York County Chapter of the Maine Organic Foods Association (later the Maine Organic Farmers and Gardeners Association or MOFGA). Mort suggested that meetings should be "more interesting." He was elected Director. Shortly thereafter he attended the first statewide meeting of the organization. He apparently did not learn his lesson, spoke again, and was nominated President. He declined then, but accepted the role two years later.

While writing a garden column for the York County Coast Star that promoted MOFGA, he and Barbara wrote a book, "Gardening for Independence." Reviews suggest it's a must read for any organic gardener or farmer, full of practical information and the humor borne out of one couple's introduction to homestead life.

The Mathers sold organic vegetables from their garden along with organic-ingredient baked goods to restaurants and food stores from Ogunquit to Portland. While engaged as an organic farmer, Mort served as Executive Director of Friends of Intelligent Land-use (FOIL) and helped that organization defeat a proposal to locate an oil refinery in Sanford. He was also asked to help save the ecologically-sensitive Laudholm Farm in Wells from the raging development sweeping southern Maine in the 1970s. With other key contributors, Mort set about incorporating, getting tax-exempt status and funding acquisition. Thirteen years later, when Mort left the Laudhom Trust, the organization had completed two $3 million campaigns, bought the farm, restored the buildings, begun education and research programs and built the largest trail system on the Maine coast south of Acadia National Park.

Mort didn't forget his theater interest, and started the Ogunquit Playhouse Foundation at the behest of long-time owner/producer John Lane. The newly-formed organization raised a $500,000 endowment in three years and, in 1997, title of the Playhouse passed to the Foundation.

And his environmental contributions continue. In 2000 he was the coordinating consultant for the $32 million campaign to purchase the largest conservation easement ever negotiated — for 762,000 acres of Maine's northern forest. Most recently he became Program Coordinator for a new Maine program called Farms for the Future. Its purpose is to preserve farmland by making farms more economically viable. And as Mort says, "What could be better for an environmentalist who loves farming than to be in a position to help farmers preserve farmland?"

Neil Rolde

When someone in Maine needs to know something about the history of the state or what's currently happening in Maine, Neil Rolde is often the person one turns to. He has done a great deal to capture and record our history and is author of nine books. His titles include "Maine, A Narrative History," "An Illustrated History of Maine," and "So You Think You Know Maine." He received the Neal W. Allen History Award in 1998 from the Maine Historical Society in recognition of "The Baxters of Maine," a biography of Governor Percival Baxter and his father James Phinney Baxter. His latest book, "The Interrupted Forest," a history of the Maine Woods, has been newly released.

Given all Neil's research and historical writings, you might expect him to be a highly academic person. You would be surprised to know perhaps that this genial and generous person spends more of his time making Maine history than recording it. He has unflagging energy and broad interests that have taken him into various arenas where he has made endless contributions. In public life Neil served as an assistant to Governor Kenneth Curtis from 1966 to 1972. In that capacity he was in charge of the re-organization of the State government into what is essentially its present Governor's Cabinet form. He also worked on key environmental legislation including two landmark bills, the Site Selection Law and the Oil Conveyance Law. The Site Selection Law set up a Board of Environmental Protection, finally providing the State with a legal mechanism to address proposed high-impact developments such as coastal refineries. The Oil Conveyance Law mandated that oil companies underwrite a contingency fund for any environmental degradation that could result from the pipeline transportation of oil through Maine to Canadian markets. These laws were passed despite fierce opposition from powerful lobbies and, in time, went on to receive national recognition.

Neil subsequently served eight terms (1972-76; 1978-90) in the Maine House of Representatives. While in the Legislature he served as Majority Leader in the House, House Chair of the Audit and Program Review Committee and member of the Education, Natural Resources and Human Services committees.

Neil also gives generously of his time and expertise to the private, non-profit world. He recently completed the maximum term possible as Chair of the Board of the Maine Public Broadcasting Corporation in Bangor and is completing his permitted tenure as Chair of the Board of the Bigelow Laboratory for Ocean Sciences in West Boothbay. He also serves on many other boards dealing with issues of health, environment, training and employment, but seems to be particularly fond of his affiliation with The SALT Institute in Portland. The SALT Institute documents and tells the many and varied stories of the people of Maine. Neil's special affection is understandable, as The SALT Institute seems to complete the circle back to Neil's love of Maine's history.

When Neil moved to Maine as a young man, he saw "so many things that could be improved if people just got together." There is no question that Neil has gotten together with a lot of people and, as a result, a lot of things have improved.

So, if you ever need to learn something about Maine history, you might well take a page from one of Neil's books. And, if you ever think you're too busy to make a contribution, you definitely should "take a page from his book."

Rosalyne S. Bernstein

Few Mainers have contributed so much to that which is not so visible and, at the same time, to that which is most visible. Rosalyne Bernstein's contributions to education and government on one hand, and the visual arts on the other, make her one of those special people.

Rosalyne says that she loves Maine because it is large enough to be interesting and varied, yet small enough to make a difference. In Rosalyne's five decades in Maine this graceful and gracious lady has made quite a difference. In the field of education she served as President of the (Portland) Roosevelt PTA and on the School Board, improving the curriculum and upgrading teacher quality. In the 1960s she co-founded the Portland public schools Headstart Program — reaching the most deprived and pioneering what was to become a broad federal program.

Outside the municipal realm, she was Maine delegate (1976-86) to the New England Board of Higher Education, serving on task forces for Higher Education and Legal Education & the New England Economy. Rosalyne also was the first woman member of the Rhodes Scholarship Committee for Maine (1976-81), a member of the University of Maine System Commission on Pluralism (1989-90) and was the first woman Overseer (1973-81) and Trustee (1981-97) of Bowdoin College. Additionally, she is a member and former Chair (1999-01) of the Board of Visitors for the University of Southern Maine and currently serves on the Board of Visitors for the University of Maine School of Law.

As much as Rosalyne is committed to education, she is equally committed to government. In recent years she has served as Chair for the Task Force to Restructure the Maine Health Care Program (1991-2) and as the Health & Social Services Co-Chair (1992-3) for the Blue Ribbon Commission to Restructure State Government. From there she was part of the Team to Implement Restructuring of Maine Departments of Human Services and Mental Health, which she chaired from 1993-4. From 1988 to 1996 she was also Chair of the Maine Health Care Finance Commission, the state agency charged with cost containment and data collection for Maine hospitals. In 2000 she served as a member of the Commission on Tax Exempt Bonding, and is currently a Board member of the Maine Educational Loan Authority.

With all Rosalyne has done in the fields of education and government, it's hard to believe that she has made an equal contribution in the visual arts world — but that's just what she has done. Rosalyne's instinctive and enthusiastic love of fine art led her to serve as a Portland School (later Maine College) of Art Trustee from 1966 to 1988. She is also a major contributor to the Portland Museum of Art, where she assumed a Trustee role (1965-93 and 97) and was President during the critical years (1979-81) when $11 million for the present Charles Shipman Payson Building was raised. With this effort, Rosalyne and her fellow Trustees turned a small insular organization into a major museum and, in so doing, helped restore the economic and cultural vitality of Portland. Today, her love of art continues and she remains Chair of the Museum's Collection Committee.

If some day you see an object of beauty in the Portland Museum of Art, perhaps it will extend your vision to what you might contribute — and, in your way, add to what Rosalyne Bernstein has contributed.

Hauntings, Ghosts & Spirits

Photo by Jim Carter

Maine has a fascinating and long history filled with stories of courage and bravery, skullduggery and cowardice, good folks and, well, some not so good. It can come as no surprise, therefore, that the tales that have survived down through the centuries include many that are mysterious, unexplainable and, sometimes, downright frightening. When you visit Maine, you'll probably hear some of these stories, and you may even meet some of the spirits and ghosts who inspire them and haunt many places throughout the state.

A prevailing theme of the many books that have been written about ghosts and the supernatural, as having occurred in Maine, is that as people met untimely, often violent and almost universally sad deaths, their spirits were somehow caught between the world we know and the world "beyond." It's often as though they left something unfinished, unattended to or unfulfilled in this life. Possibly as a result, they remain inexplicably suspended in an in-between state, a limbo world into which we are rarely able to see, if ever so hazily. And yet, frequently there are sightings, some piece of evidence — an apparition, a sound, a voice, a chill in the air, a strange odor, a feeling, and yes, even a thump in the night — some convincing indication that something we can't explain is definitely here with us, making its presence known for what purpose we cannot fathom. Perhaps seeking some kind of closure, defending sacred turf, perhaps giving warning or just seeking empathy — spirits and ghosts leave those that experience their presence with more questions than answers, but absolutely certain that what they have witnessed was an encounter of the supernatural kind.

"Pitcher Man"

In Goose River you may find yourself among the many who have seen the essence of William Richardson, who was killed there in 1783. Richardson, who had become something of a local hero in the struggle with the British, was celebrating the signing of the Treaty of Paris with friends and neighbors, eventually roaming around the village with a pitcher of ale offering to share it with anyone and everyone. He is said to have encountered three men on horseback near the bridge across the river, and offered to share his pitcher with them, not realizing in his inebriated state that they were Tories, and unhappy ones at that. Their response to his kindness was a brutal rifle butt to Richardson's head, which not only ended his celebration, but his life (and, perhaps worst of all, likely spilled the ale, as well). Those who have encountered Richardson near the bridge, even in recent years, consistently report that he is still holding — and offering — his pitcher, which is why he is known as the "pitcher man" ghost. If he offers you a drink, you might want to carefully consider your response — he might still be angry about the whole thing.

Haunted Lighthouses

Maine's lighthouses — "America's castles" — are a likely venue for ghosts, and many are said to be haunted, no surprise in as much as many a keeper witnessed tragedy or even personally suffered an untimely demise. Add to that the remote location, often excruciating loneliness, the helplessness and the absence of neighbors, friends, family and community, and you have a perfect setting for the reaping of spooky tales.

The Seguin Lighthouse, off Popham Beach, is said to be the residence of at least two ghosts. The "Old Captain," as he is popularly known, is thought to be the keeper who, in the mid-1800s, did his wife in after she allegedly drove him insane by playing the same melody incessantly on her piano. He did himself in, as well, but is still often seen climbing up the spiral stairs to the tower, presumably to tend the light. He also was reportedly seen by Coast Guard personnel during the 1980s when he stood behind a player in a game of checkers, presumably watching the game's progress.

On another occasion, this one also experienced by Coast Guardsmen in recent years, the "Old Captain" apparently was displeased when, as the light was being automated, the furnishings in the keeper's house were being removed. The ghost paid a middle-of-the-night visit to the officer in charge, shook his bed violently and said, "Don't take the furniture." Of course the project went ahead anyway, and the household items were loaded into the dory the following day, to be lowered carefully by winch to the water's edge and then rowed to the mainland. Something went awry, however, as the winch motor froze, the chain broke and the dory, furniture and all, went plummeting down the track and into the sea, sinking with the loss of the entire cargo. The officer reportedly needed no convincing as to who was responsible for the highly-unlikely mishap.

As for his wife, many a passing ship's crew has heard her piano being played, always the same tune, as they pass by in the night.

A third ghost, that of a young girl, has also been sighted frequently on the island, and has even laughed and waved to those who have seen her. Such a child is reported to have died mysteriously on the island many years ago, and was buried there. Before you cancel your visit to the Seguin Light, however, it should be noted that none of these spirits has exhibited any malice toward those who have recently witnessed their appearances.

Many local fishermen are certain that there's a ghost on Ram Island Light, off the harbor near Portland. There have been countless times in foul weather when they have been warned off by a loud whistle coming from the island — even though there is no whistle at Ram Island Light. On other occasions, they have been alerted to the danger of the island's shoals by fires on the shore at the water's edge, but subsequent investigations have revealed no residue or other evidence of the fires there. The fishermen give credit to the man who was shipwrecked on the island in the mid 1800s, and who perished there from exposure and starvation.

Terror in the Night

Not all of Maine's ghosts inhabit lighthouses, of course. And not all are quite so amiable. A boy named Ben Bennett was brutally murdered — beheaded with a single swipe of a large knife — when he and some friends accidentally came across a band of rum-runners unloading their contraband in Port Clyde in the early 1900s. The other boys managed to flee to tell the story, and the outlaws escaped after throwing their victim's body into a swamp near the shore. Townspeople have many times since reported seeing a large man with a big knife chasing a terrified boy, both of whom then disappear into the mists. Several people have actually been chased (but, fortunately, not caught) by the man with the knife. In all cases, witnesses report that the man's boots neither make any sound nor leave tracks as he runs over the terrain. Others have seen the boy, alone, hovering above the swamp along the lighthouse road. So when you're in the area and you notice someone following you without leaving footprints or making any sounds, well....

Hendrick's Head Light near Southport may be another place to chase down a ghost; it is supposedly one of the most haunted lighthouses in New England. Many sailors have died on the rocks and in the sea nearby, and make their presence known in a variety of ways. The most prominent among the ghosts here, however, is that of a young woman who, according to the story, was last seen alive walking along the shore near the lighthouse — all alone, a complete stranger, attractive and somewhat mysterious.

She was found the following day washed up on the beach, drowned, a girdle of weights strapped around her waist. No one knows if she jumped or was pushed. Indeed, no one has ever learned her identity, let alone why she was there in the first place. All they know is that she is often still seen walking on the beach near the lighthouse, troubled and as if lost, leaving footprints (at least this ghost carries some weight) in the sand that suggest that she's wandering about with neither aim nor destination.

Ghosts Aplenty

A visit to the Isles of Shoals, that collection of tiny islands off the coast at the southern border of Maine, will bring you to the home of several ghosts. Some have been seen so often and so consistently that the places where they appear have been named for them.

There is Betty Moody's Cave, for example, where she and her daughter hid trying to evade marauding Indians in 1724. While they weren't successful, they are still seen there from time to time. The same is true of Babb's Cove and Miss Underhill's chair, the latter a ledge of rocks from which Nancy Underhill drowned in the sea.

There's also the sad, eerie crying of a woman that has been heard by many approximately two hours before a storm strikes the Isles of Shoals, as if to warn mariners of the oncoming danger.

The Isles of Shoals has been the scene of many a dastardly deed, including at least one notorious murder. Many speculate that it is the victims who are responsible for uncounted instances of apparitions, moving furniture, crying, moaning, foul odors, cold spots, footsteps and other sounds, all in locations devoid of human presence.

If you're fortunate and persistent, you might encounter the "Pirate's Bride" there, a beautiful young woman who was left behind when one of Blackbeard's cohorts returned to sea after allegedly burying his treasure on Appledore. He made her swear to wait for him, which she faithfully did, but he never came back for her. Now she roams the cliffs, looking out to sea, and is usually seen early in the morning. She has on a number of occasions answered visitors' questions, always with the same words: "He will come back." Reports consistently describe her in almost the same words, and assert that her footsteps make no sound on the shell-strewn sand.

Haunted Houses

There are, as you might expect, many houses in Maine with ghostly and spiritual dwellers. If you know where to look, you may well find one...assuming that's what you would like to do.

There's the Forder House on the Fore River in Westbrook in which an apparition of a woman, called "the woman in the shawl," has appeared many times over the years. More often than not, she is seen standing at an upstairs bedroom window, looking out across the water. Records indicate that the Lodbell family, living in the house in 1799, bore and lost twin boys, which understandably brought profound sadness to Mary, their mother.

A young couple recently living in a two-century-old house in Norway discovered that it was haunted by a spirit that seemed to protect their infant son. This unseen force physically lifted their newborn out of the crib and laid him safely on the floor on several occasions, and literally hurled the family's pet cat out of the room when it got too close to the child. The couple subsequently learned that the house had once been occupied by a family whose infant son suffocated in his crib (with the family cat asleep alongside him).

Not all ghosts are so accommodating, of course. A group of young people living in an old house in Orrington were essentially harassed to the point of moving out by a spirit or spirits who not only moved furniture and other items, opened and closed windows, stoked fires and frightened pets, but literally wrote messages such as "get out" in pencil on the walls, even newly-painted ones, throughout the house. They eventually complied.

Tales of haunted houses have entertained folks since time began, no doubt, but one, in Northport, has a particularly unique slant.

The home of Mr. and Mrs. Edward Cosgrove was lavishly expansive — its owners were wealthy and, if their two Cadillacs and their Rolls Royce were any indication, somewhat ostentatious. They hired an elderly couple, Walden was their name, to watch over and tend to their three children, which was the case when the parents went to Boston for some Christmas shopping on Dec. 16, 1954.

A fire of unknown origin burned the house to the ground that night, save for its two chimneys, and all three children and the care-taking couple died in the conflagration. The remorseful Cosgroves sold the land and moved away, and subsequent owners never rebuilt on that exact location on the grounds, but allowed the two chimneys to remain, perhaps out of respect and in tribute to the tragedy that had taken place there.

Many people, including a local minister, have subsequently reported hearing the children crying and screaming in panic at the ruins of the house. But the strangest event took place when a young couple happened on the site by chance and, curious, took photographs of the crumbling chimneys. When they got their pictures back, they were shocked to see perfectly clear and real photos of the huge white house, in tact as it originally stood, its chimneys in the appropriate locations.

Assuming some mistake by the film developers, they checked, only to find that there had been no mistake. No mix-up. Nor has there ever been any explanation for the phenomenon.

Helping Hands

There's reportedly a ghost you might encounter when you visit the Owls Head Lighthouse that you might like to take home with you. According to the lore, the ghost is that of a former light keeper who died on duty, his task unfulfilled. Subsequent keepers have reported a number of incidents in which they found his footprints going up the ramp from the keeper's house to the light tower — but never any coming back down. They have found locked doors opened and signs that someone had tended to the lens — i.e., the brass has been polished to a luster when no one has been present.

Owls Head is also the home of a ghost called the "Little Lady," most noted because her apparition is that of a happy, kindly, beautiful woman. During her visits, which usually occur between 11pm and 1am, according to reports, all present feel a sense of joy and calm. She might also be welcome in many homes.

Friendly Ghosts

Sarah Whitesell, the lovely 11-year-old girl who fell to her death from the trail atop Mt. Megunticook while on a family outing in May of 1864 is still seen by hikers from time to time near where she died. Dressed in her original clothes, she is still smiling, seemingly enjoying the fresh flowers, the clean mountain air and the spectacular view of the lake and Camden Hills below.

She is reportedly a non-threatening presence, emitting a happy, warm, even friendly glow. The locals avoid picking "her" flowers, and urge you to do the same when you visit "Maiden's Cliff."

By contrast, some ghosts are just downright nasty — even if they happen to be relatives.

A woman in Bethel was confronted by the image of her own great-grandfather when she dared to approach him in what was originally his house and even dared to stay in his bedroom (the one in which he died). Other relatives who have braved a stay in that room have reported being awakened, feeling that something was choking them, but have been able to fight off whatever the force and escape. It's always a good idea keep peace in the family.

Good Witch, Bad Witch

Mary Nasson lived in York in the mid-1700s, and became knowledgeable in the medicinal uses of herbs at an early age. Even as a child, she helped her friends heal scrapes and bruises with the use of the emollients she extracted from her garden.

By the time she reached adulthood, she was regarded as a "white magic" healer and, eventually, even an exorcist. Her notoriety grew when she was called to rid a neighbor's home of an evil spirit and, following a harrowing all-night vigil, was successful. After that episode, some started to regard her as a witch.

Following her death at the age of 29, Mary's reputation continued to grow when children playing in her yard reported being "pushed" on her swings when no one was near. Flowers were said to pick themselves and collect at the edge of her garden. Nonetheless, because she was generally regarded as a witch, when she was buried a huge slab of stone was placed over her grave, supposedly as a way to keep her inside. You can visit her unique grave, with both headstone and footstone at either end of the granite slab, in the Old Burying Ground cemetery in York Village. It's right in the middle of town, across from Town Hall and part of the museum properties of the Old York Historical Society.

The Sayward-Wheeler House in York, the restored home of a wealthy 17th-century merchant, is also the residence of a ghost, who watches over the antique furnishings and museum-quality collections in the house. The house is a property under the care of the Society for the Preservation of New England Antiquities (SPNEA), is open to the public and is sometimes the setting for genteel teas and parties. It was at one of the latter that the ghost made one of its most memorable appearances.

It seems the ghost took a disliking to one of the guests, a prominent attorney and politician (and a thoroughly likable fellow). While the gentleman was engaged in conversation with several other guests, the ghost lifted up his cup and poured its contents down his shirt and tie, then replaced the cup on its saucer. Whether the victim or those around him were more shocked seemed of little matter — the ghost had the last word.

The Music Plays On

In Boothbay Harbor, an old upright piano was for many years the only reminder of the second-floor occupants of what is known as the Boothbay Opera House (a building that has housed many things over many years, but never an opera). The room was the meeting place of the Knights of Pythias, and was the scene of many a celebration and party, at which the piano was often the centerpiece for revelers.

One piano player, Earl Cliff, is still remembered as having been particularly good (he was known as Earl "Fingers" Cliff). Fingers Cliff was apparently at the top of his game at a two-day party the Knights celebrated in the fall of 1907, and old-timers there have talked about it for decades. And they have occasional reminders: The piano plays what many believe are Cliff's old tunes from time to time when nobody is at the keyboard. Many have witnessed it, and have tried to explain it away, without success. No one is certain it's ole' Fingers himself, but no one is arguing, either, and today you can visit Boothbay Harbor's very own Phantom of the Opera.

Nordica Auditorium at the University of Maine in Farmington is believed to be haunted by its namesake, the wonderful Lillian Nordica, the Farmington native considered the premier opera singer of the 19th century.

And if you like scary movies, you might want to check out the Skowhegan Cinema, where ghostly hauntings have caused the owners considerable anguish.

Household furnishings have also been known to be haunted in Maine. A man in Waterboro found, after moving to four different houses to escape a ghost, that an antique table he had inherited was the source of nighttime thumping and pounding that kept the family awake and, often, terrified as well. He finally sold the table to an unsuspecting antiques dealer who later reported that he, too, had experienced the pounding noise from time to time, and hadn't been able to figure out the source.

So when you visit Maine, keep in mind that there is more than meets the eye sometimes, and often more than can be explained scientifically. It's all part of what makes this great state so appealing.

If you come across an antique table that you find absolutely irresistible, however, just make sure you check out its history before you buy it and take it home.

The Best Hiking & Walking Tours

Hikers on Mt. Katahdin, by John Brough

One of the best ways to get acquainted with the real Maine is to stop, leave the car behind and explore it on foot. In the villages and small cities you can stroll through history and revel in the unique architecture, beautifully-maintained homes and historic sites like gemstones in wondrous natural settings. In the rural areas, your reward is a moose's-eye view of some of the most spectacular country on the planet and a highlight of your visit that you'll treasure. You don't have to be a mountain-climber to enjoy most of the state's trails and paths — just a willingness to stop and sense the fields of wildflowers — and trees and meadows and wildlife and glacial outcroppings and rugged seacoast — that await you.

Greater Portland

• Portland Trails — Portland (urban, easy)
Portland Trails, a nonprofit organization, is in the process of creating a 30-mile network of trails throughout the greater Portland area. Included are trails along the Eastern Promenade with dramatic views of Casco Bay, the Audubon Society's Fore River Sanctuary, the Baxter Woods, the Back Cove and the vibrant waterfront. Open year round. Stop by for a free map.
More Info: Portland Trails, 1 India Street, Portland, ME 04101

(207) 775-2411
www.trails.org
email:info@trails.org

Midcoast

• Salt Bay Preserve Heritage Trail — Pemaquid Peninsula (rural, easy)
   A short three-mile path across a salt marsh and mud flat. See the ancient oyster shell middens of early Native Americans. These Glidden Middens date back over 2000 years and are included in the National Register of Historic Places. They are protected by federal law and should not be disturbed.
   From Route 1 in Damariscotta, north on Mills Road (ME 215) for about one mile on right side. Maps can be found at trailhead.

• Rockport (urban, easy)
   The three-mile loop through this beautiful village takes you past historic lime kilns, gorgeous yachts, gardens and an outdoor chapel overlooking Penobscot Bay. At the town landing, a statue of Andre the Seal recalls this frequent and popular summer visitor to Rockport. Be sure to check out the interesting shops and businesses often found in buildings built with large blocks of granite from the native quarry.
   From Camden go south on Route 1. Turn left on Pascal Avenue and continue straight for four miles until you see the harbor on your left. On your left you will see a sign for Cramer Park and parking area. This is the trailhead.
More Info: Rockport-Camden-Lincolnville Chamber of Commerce, PO Box 919M, Camden, ME 04843
(207) 236-4404

• Fernald's Neck — Camden area (close to urban setting, easy-to-moderate)
   This five-mile hike takes you on a peninsula jutting out into scenic Megunticook Lake. The Nature Conservancy is holder of this beautiful preserve of freshwater bog, cliffs and glacially-deposited boulders.
   From Camden head north on ME 52 to Youngtown Corner. From the corner bear left and look for a sign marking Fire Road 50, opposite highway marker 5016. Turn down Fire Road 50 and go past the Hattie Lamb Fernald section of the preserve, which is on your left. Turn left at the fork in the road. If conditions permit, continue down this gravel road and through the hayfield. The parking area is at the trailhead.
More Info: Maine Chapter, The Nature Conservancy, Fort Andross, 14 Maine Street, Suite 401, Brunswick, ME 04011
(207) 729-5181

• Mts. Battie & Megunticook — Camden area (close to urban setting, moderate)

This four-mile trip takes you to two summits, each affording panoramic views of Penobscot Bay and the beautiful town of Camden. Follow the Mt. Battie Trail to the Tableland Trail to the Ridge Trail. Mt. Megunticook is the highest of the Camden Hills at 1,385 feet above sea level.

In Camden take Route 1 to ME 52 north and west. Take the first right, Megunticook Street and follow to its end. At the top of a small drive there is a parking area. The Mt. Battie Trail begins there.

More Info: Camden Hills State Park, Camden, ME 04843, or Bureau of Parks and Recreation, Maine Department of Conservation, State House Station 22, Augusta, ME 04333

(207) 289-3821

• Bald Rock Mountain — Camden Hills State Park (close to urban setting, moderate)

A trip of three-and-one-half miles up Bald Rock Mountain affords mostly very private hiking. The views from the summit of Islesboro, Lincolnville Beach and Deer Isle are spectacular. Notice how hardwood species give way to evergreens as you climb.

From Camden take Route 1 to ME 173 east. Go three miles on ME 173 and turn left at junction with Youngtown Road. The parking lot is on your immediate left. The trailhead begins at the parking lot.

More Info: Camden Hills State Park, Camden, ME 04843, Bureau of Parks and Recreation, Maine Department of Conservation, State House Station 22, Augusta, ME 04333

(207) 289-3821

• Maiden Cliff above Megunticook Lake — Camden area (close to urban setting, easy)

Take this short two-mile trip up the 800 feet of Maiden Cliff for a beautiful view of Megunticook Lake. From this rocky outcropping you can even see features of the lake below the surface. Note the wooden cross that marks where an 11-year-old girl fell to her death in 1864.

From Camden go about three miles west on ME 52. Parking area is on right side where the trailhead is located.

• Islesboro — island off Lincolnville (easy)

Walk into a gentler time of stately homes and manicured grounds. Stroll five miles of quiet roads with ocean views never more than a glance away. Pendleton Point affords magnificent views of the ocean and islands of Penobscot Bay.

From Lincolnville Beach take the ferry to Islesboro Island. From the landing, by car or bike, take Ferry Road and turn right at the first intersection. Follow this road to its intersection with Main Road. Turn right on to Main Road and proceed to Dark Harbor, which is the trailhead.

More Info: Islesboro Town Office, Main Road, Islesboro, ME 04848
(207) 734-2253

• Monhegan — island off Port Clyde (moderate)

Hike this magnificent Atlantic outpost a short but awe-inspiring 1.5 miles. Find tranquillity in the virgin Cathedral Woods and breathtaking views of the ocean from the headlands.

Take the ferry from Boothbay Harbor or Port Clyde. From the landing locate the Cathedral Woods Trail, then the Cliff Trail.

More Info: A boat schedule from Port Clyde is available from Monhegan Boat Line, PO Box 238, Port Clyde, ME 04855 (207) 372-8848

A summer boat schedule from Boothbay Harbor is available from Balmy Days, Boothbay Harbor, ME 04538
(207) 633-2284

Down East

• Acadia Mountain & East Summit — Acadia National Park (moderate)

This trip of two-plus miles takes you to the twin summits of 681 and 646 feet. You will be rewarded with wonderful views of Somes Sound, the only true fjord on the East Coast, the North Atlantic and other mountains of Acadia National Park.

From Somesville take ME 102 south to the Acadia Mountain parking area on the right side of the road. The parking area is the trailhead.

• Blue Hill (rural, easy-moderate)

This two-mile trip takes you to the top of Blue Hill at an elevation of 934 feet. It offers wonderful views of Penobscot Bay, the Camden Hills, the mountains of Mount Desert and Blue Hill Bay. On a very clear day you might be able to see Mt. Washington in the New Hampshire White Mountains.

From Ellsworth take Route 1 toward Bucksport. In East Orland turn left onto ME 15 (Blue Hill Road). Continue for about 11 miles and look for Mountain Road on the left. Follow Mountain Road for about 4/10th mile and look for the fire tower trail sign that marks the trailhead.

• Castine (urban, easy)

Historic Castine village on Penobscot Bay offers a wonderful one-to-two-mile stroll through American history. You can see beautiful 18th- and 19th-century homes and churches, Fort George State Park, Dice Head Light and much more, highlighted by historical markers. If it's not on sea duty, be sure to see The State of Maine, the 500-foot training vessel of Castine's Maine Maritime Academy.

From Bucksport take Route 1 east to Orland and turn right on to Route 175 (Castine Road). Follow ME 175 to West Penobscot, then south on ME 166. At the junction of ME 166 and ME 166A, bear right onto ME 166A. Follow the signs to Castine. Drive onto the peninsula and follow ME 166 to Battle Avenue. Proceed on Battle Avenue and turn left onto Main Street. The parking area is at the bottom of the hill. This is also the trailhead.

More Info: Castine Merchants Association, PO Box 329 Castine, ME 04421

• Peaked Mountain — Penobscot County (rural, moderate)

This two-and-one-half-mile trail takes you through an old forest road, then up a steep climb to a rocky peak. The peak is exposed granite that can be seen for miles around. From the peak you have commanding views of Mount Katahdin to the northwest, the mountains of Mount Desert Island to the southeast and the Penobscot River to the north.

From Brewer go east on ME 9 to East Eddington. Continue through East Eddington to the intersection with ME 180 on your right. Continue on ME 9 for another three miles and look for the campground at Parks Pond on the right. Turn north across from the campground. A little more than one mile brings you to a graveled parking area, which is where the trailhead is located.

• Reversing Falls Park — near Pembroke, Washington County (rural, easy)

A trek of less than one mile takes you out a peninsula where you can see the powerful Bay of Fundy tides at work. Spend some time watching and you will see whirlpools, rips and a roaring waterfall that reverses itself at high tide.

From Dennysville, head north on Route 1 and turn right at the Triangle Grocery in Pembroke. Drive a short distance and turn right by the Odd Fellows Hall and follow Leighton Neck Road. Turn at the third, unmarked intersection from the right. After turning, pass a cemetery on the right and go down a steep hill. At the head of a small cove turn left. Continue on the road to where it turns to gravel. After about six miles you will come to a turnaround at the Reversing Falls Park. The parking area is where the trailhead is located.

• Quoddy Head State Park — near Lubec (rural, easy-moderate)

This short hike of about one mile takes you to the candy-striped West Quoddy Head Light. You can see Grand Manan Island close by in Canada. A special treat is Gulliver's Hole, a roaring sea cave. Walk with rocks and waves directly beneath you.

From Route 1 in Whiting head east on ME 189 by a sign for Quoddy Head State Park. Go a little more than nine miles on ME 189 toward Lubec and turn right by the gas station at the intersection of South Lubec Road. Follow the road to the parking area at West Quoddy Head. The parking area is where the trailhead is located.

• Crockett Cove Woods — Hancock County (rural, easy)
A trail and loop of 1.5 miles preserved by The Nature Conservancy brings you through a damp but beautiful woods where fog abounds. Mosses and lichen cover trees, rocks and glacial boulders. Walk on planks over a boggy area of sphagnum moss and exotic pitcher plants.
From Blue Hill take ME 15 south to Deer Isle. At Deer Isle Village turn right onto Sunset. Turn right again onto Whitman Road, about three miles from the Sunset post office. Look for Fire Lane 88 on your right. Follow the fire lane to a small parking lot where the trailhead and registration box are located.

• Pineo Ridge — Washington County (remote, open walk, easy)
This is a completely discretionary walk across a vast expanse. This blueberry barren is a glacial plain and features kettle holes formed by the pressure of vast blocks of ice left after the glacier passed. Blueberry bushes have been planted everywhere, interspersed with pines planted to retard erosion.
From the south on Route 1, cross the Narraguagus River in Cherryfield. Just past the bridge, take first left and head north on ME 193. After about one mile take the surfaced road to the right. Continue on it for about five miles. After passing a warning sign about honeybees, take a left at the fork. Park off the road; this is the trailhead.

• Isle Au Haut — island off Stonington, part of Acadia National Park (easy)
This five-mile hike takes you through a less traveled part of the Acadia National Park. Escape out to sea and combine evergreen forest and seaside walks.
From Stonington take the ferry to the town landing. Turn right to the ranger station. At the ranger station, take the Duck Harbor Trail.
More Info: Acadia National Park, Bar Harbor, ME 04609
(207) 288-3338

Kennebec & Moose River Valleys

• Skowhegan (urban, easy)
This four-mile trip along the Kennebec River is a walk through Revolutionary War history. See the famous falls that General Benedict Arnold had

to contend with as his men portaged their heavy boats around them during the expedition to Quebec. View the river from the Coburn Park bluffs and visit the beautiful stone Dame De Lourdes Church.

From the south, take I-95 through Waterville to exit 36. Take U.S. Highway 201 north to Hinckley, then turn right on ME 23. Cross the Kennebec River at Pishon Ferry and go north to the junction of U.S. Highway 2 in Canaan. Turn left on U.S. 2 and continue to Skowhegan. In the town look for a sign reading the "Kennebec Banks Rest Area" on the left. Park at the Kennebec Banks. This is the trailhead.

More Info: Skowhegan Chamber of Commerce, Municipal Parking Lot, Skowhegan, ME 04976
(207) 474-3621

Moosehead Lake & Katahdin

• Mount Katahdin along the Knife Edge Trail — Baxter State Park (remote, difficult, potentially hazardous)

A full-day hike via a nine-mile loop to Baxter Peak at 5,267 feet and the northern terminus of the Appalachian Trail. This hike provides spectacular views of Moosehead Lake and the Penobscot River as well as the mountains of Acadia National Park and Camden Hills State Park.

From Millinocket, follow signs to Baxter State Park and enter the Park at Togue Pond; bear right to the Roaring Brook Campground. The hike begins at the ranger station where you sign in and out.

More Info: Baxter State Park , 65 Balsam Drive, Millinocket, ME 04462
(207) 723-5140

• Mount Kineo-Moosehead Lake — Somerset County (rural, easy-to-moderate)

A unique four-mile hike that begins by boat. Mount Kineo is 1,780 feet above sea level in the middle of spectacular Moosehead Lake. The climb offers a panoramic view of the lake and wonderful vistas of Maine's big woods.

Take Routes 6 & 15 to Rockwood. Either launch your own craft from the public landing or locate a local outfitter or water taxi to take you to the trailhead.

More Info: Moosehead Lake Region Chamber of Commerce, PO Box 581, Greenville, ME 04441
(207) 695-2702

• Caribou Bog — Penobscot County (close to urban setting, easy)

A 10-mile walk through woodland and freshwater marshes. This walk provides abundant opportunity to see songbirds, waterfowl and to possibly spot deer, foxes and coyotes.

From Bangor take Stillwater Avenue north to Orono and the intersection of Forest Avenue. Turn left onto Forest and park on the right. The trail begins on the other side of the road.

Far North

• Aroostook State Park — near Presque Isle (easy-to-moderate)
An unusual one-plus-mile trip up twin peaks of an extinct volcano. Views of Maine's potato fields and the woodlands of Maine's largest county — Aroostook. Look for evidence of an ancient sea and volcanic activity.
Take Route 1 north to Aroostook County. About 10 miles north of Mars Hill follow signs to Aroostook State Park. From the campground take the North-South Peak Trail.
More Info: Aroostook State Park, 87 State Park Road, Presque Isle, ME 04769 (207) 768-8341

Historic Sites

Sayward-Wheeler House, York, by Jim Carter

Many of the most interesting and educational places in Maine are well off the beaten track, often where historically-significant events occurred or, in some cases, where notable people lived or worked. Many are of museum quality. Here are those we consider the best.

Southern Coastal

• Hamilton House — South Berwick
A beautiful house overlooking the Salmon Falls River, built by merchant Jonathan Hamilton in 1787. Refurbished to reflect its original character and ambiance.
40 Vaughn's Lane, South Berwick, ME 03908
(207) 384-2454
www.SPNEA.org

• Old York Historical Society — York
Beautifully-restored and preserved museum homes and buildings in York Village and along the York River, where America's first chartered city (1652) was settled more than 370 years ago (1632). Among them is the Old Gaol, one of the

oldest public buildings in America still in existence, Jefferds' Tavern, the John Hancock Warehouse and the Elizabeth Perkins House. Collections, furnishings and artifacts (such as the Bulman Bedhangings, the only complete set of crewel bedhangings to have survived from the 18th century) reflect the town's rich heritage. Generally regarded as one of the finest society exhibits in New England.
207 York Street, York, ME 03909
(207) 363-4974
www.oldyork.org
email: oyhs@oldyork.org

• Sayward-Wheeler House — York
    Built in 1718 as the family home of a wealthy merchant, and maintained with its original furnishings. Overlooking York Harbor and the York River. Maintained by the Society for the Preservation of New England Antiquities.
Barrell Lane Extension, York, ME 03909
(603) 436-3205
www.SPNEA.org

• Sarah Orne Jewett House — South Berwick
    The author's home, the place where she wrote during the late 19th century, and one often reflected in her works. Built in 1774 in Georgian style by a wealthy sea captain. Refurbished to reflect the author's décor.
5 Portland Street, South Berwick, ME 03908
(207) 384-2454
www.SPNEA.org

• Fort McClary State Historic Site — Kittery
    Buildings on this historic site represent the five wars — from the Revolutionary War to World War I — during which this fort was active. A splendid view of the harbor, as well.
Kittery Point Road, Kittery, ME 03904
(207) 384-6160 (winter)

• Willowbrook at Newfield — Newfield
    New England's largest fully-restored 19th-century museum village — 37 buildings and over 10,000 artifacts, including over 60 horse-drawn sleighs and carriages, an 1894 Concord stagecoach and a fully-restored, animated 1894 Armitage-Herschell carousel.
Elm Street, PO Box 80, Newfield, ME 04056
(207) 793-2784

Greater Portland

• Victoria Mansion — Portland
    Built in 1858, this is a fine example of Italian villa architecture. On exhibit are 90 percent of the original furnishings (but no secrets).
(207) 772-4841
www.portlandarts.com
email: victoria@maine.rr.com

• Tate House — Portland
    A beautiful colonial house built in 1755 by the man in America charged with supplying masts for the ships of the British Navy. Recently restored and enhanced by historically-inspired landscaping and an 18th-century herb garden.
((207) 774-9781
www.tatehouse.org

• Wadsworth-Longfellow House — Portland
    The brick colonial home where Henry Wadsworth Longfellow grew up, built in 1785. Original furnishings and a beautiful, quiet garden make it easy to understand the poet's inspiration.
(207) 772-1807
www.mainehistory.org

Western Mountains & Lakes

• Doctor Moses Mason House — Bethel
    The headquarters of the Bethel Historical Society, built in 1813, noted for its murals by Rufus Porter.
(207) 824-2908
1-800-824-2910

• Norlands Living History Center — Livermore Falls
    The family home of the Washburns, an important American political dynasty. Five historic buildings on a 445-acre farm offer hands-on living history experiences in 19th-century rural life in Maine.
290 Norlands Road, Livermore Falls, ME 04253
(207) 897-4366
www.norlands.org

Midcoast

• Joshua Chamberlain House — Brunswick
   The residence of Maine's legendary Gettysburg hero features its original furnishings along with a display of Civil War memorabilia (even the boots the great man wore during the battle).
(207) 729-6606

• Castle Tucker & Nickels-Sortwell House — Wiscasset
   These two 1807 houses, both maintained by the Society for the Preservation of New England Antiquities, would both be worth a visit even if they didn't offer beautiful original furnishings and antiques.
(207) 882-7364
www.SPNEA.org

• Montpelier — Thomaston
   General Henry Knox, George Washington's Secretary of War, made his home in this 22-room mansion, which commands its surroundings from atop a knoll just off Route 1.
(207) 354-8062
www.generalknoxmuseum.org

• Colonial Pemaquid State Historic Site — Bristol
   Extensive archaeological excavation of 14 structures from the 17th and 18th centuries and the officers' headquarters of Fort William Henry and Fort Frederick.
Colonial Pemaquid Drive, Bristol, ME 04554

• Eagle Island State Historic Park — South Harpswell
   The summer home of the famous North Pole explorer Admiral Robert E. Peary. The Peary family home is open for tours.
PO Box 161, South Harpswell, ME 04079
(207) 624-6080
www.state.me.us/doc/prkslnds/prkslnds.htm

• Fort Edgecomb State Historic Site — Edgecomb
   An octagonal 1808 blockhouse and restored fortifications overlooking the Sheepscot River. Originally built to protect the harbor in Wiscasset, then the most important shipping center north of Boston. 66 Fort Road, Edgecomb, ME 04556
(207) 882-7777 (winter)
www.state.me.us/doc/prkslnds/prkslnds.htm

• Fort Knox State Historic Site — Prospect
There's no gold stored here, but there are riches in the form of Maine's largest historic fort, complete with stunning military architecture and master granite craftsmanship. Built between 1844 and 1869 on the strategic narrows of the Penobscot River.
Route 174, Prospect, ME 04981
(207) 469-7719
http://fortknox.maineguide.com

• Fort Popham State Historic Site — Phippsburg
One of the many forts built around the mouth of the Penobscot River, this one spurred by the Civil War.
Route 209, Phippsburg, ME
(207) 389-1335
www.state.me.us/doc/prkslnds/prkslnds.htm

• Old Conway Homestead — Camden
Also known as the Meeker Cramer Museum, with several buildings, a display of antique tools, carriages and sleighs, a blacksmith shop, a maple sugar house and a restored 18th-century house.
(207) 236-2257

Down East

• Burnham Tavern — Machias
The oldest building in the Down East area. Its life as a tavern and gathering place was interrupted after the Revolutionary War's first naval battle, which was fought in the waters off the coast here, when it served as an emergency hospital. Furnished much as when it was a popular watering hole.
(207) 255-4432

• John Perkins House — Castine
This house, built in 1763, is the only pre-Revolutionary house remaining in the town. Limited access — appointment recommended.
(207) 326-8545.

• Thomas A. Hill House — Bangor
This 1836 Greek Revival home includes 19th-century furnishings and changing exhibits. The house was designed by Richard Upjohn, and serves now as the headquarters for the Bangor Historical Society.
(207) 942-5766.

• Roosevelt House — Campobello Island
FDR's sprawling summer home on scenic Campobello Island. Take the Roosevelt International Bridge.
(506) 752-2922

Kennebec & Moose River Valley

• Margaret Chase Smith Library — Skowhegan
The remarkable life and career of Senator Margaret Chase Smith is documented and reflected in this fine collection of archival and artifactual materials. The location alone is worth the trip.
54 Norridgewock Ave., Skowhegan, ME 04976
(207) 474-7133
www.mcslibrary.org
email: davidr@somtel.com

• Old Fort Western — Augusta
This fort, built in 1754 on the banks of the Kennebec River, is a National Historic Landmark.
16 Colony Street, Augusta, ME 04330
(207) 626-2385
www.oldfortwestern.org
email: oldfort@oldfortwestern.org

Far North

• Acadian Archives — Fort Kent
Collections reflecting Maine's proximity to Quebec.
University of Maine at Fort Kent
23 University Drive, Fort Kent, ME 04743
(207) 834-7536
www.umfk.maine.edu/infoserv/archives
email: acadian@maine.edu

• Maine Swedish Colony — Stockholm
Three historic sites being restored to perpetuate the history of the Swedish colony established in Maine in 1870.
RR#1, Box 41, Stockholm, ME 04783
(207) 896-5624

Unusual Learning Opportunities

Courtesy of WoodenBoat Magazine, Brooklin

Many visitors to Maine take something home with them — something of great value. Neither a beach stone nor pine cone, but knowledge — useful information and skills that enrich them for the rest of their lives. They don't find it in the places occupied by tourist throngs, but rather in places that offer special, sometimes even unique, learning experiences.

It's all part of what makes Maine so special — particularly for the discerning. Here are a few examples of what's available if you know where to look (which is what we're all about).

Southern Coastal

• Sabbathday Lake Shaker Village — New Gloucester
  Shaker Museum. Here's your chance to step back in time and make something of enduring quality. Workshops on making chairs, dovetail trays, small benches; blacksmithing; chair-caning; basket-weaving; quilting; drawing; herb-gardening; fiber arts; pressed-flower art; weaving; doll-making. Shops and crafts demonstrations. Exhibits, bookstore, gift shop, pies and other goodies. Apple Saturday Walking Tours and other special programs.
707 Shaker Road, New Gloucester, ME 04260
(207) 926-4597
www.shaker.lib.me.us
library email only: brooks1@shaker.library.me.us
office email: usshaker@aol.com

Greater Portland

• The SALT Institute for Documentary Studies — Portland
  Academic institutions are not typically in the purview of this book. However, this Institute is so unusual — and so special to Maine — that we just had to include it. It's right in downtown Portland and is the only school of its kind anywhere in the world!
  For over a quarter century, SALT has been teaching students from all over the United States how to document a region and its people. By recording the lives and work of the people of Maine, SALT students of writing and photography are allowed to practice their craft, receive academic credit and have their work published in SALT Magazine and other SALT publications. And, in the process, the living history of Maine is captured and preserved.
  Cultural journalist Pamela H. Wood founded The SALT Institute in 1973 and today it is a nonprofit organization governed by a Board of Trustees and advised by a national Academic Board. SALT offers semester-length programs in nonfiction writing and editing and documentary radio and documentary photography. Accredited programs are offered at both the undergraduate and graduate level.
PO Box 7800, 110 Exchange Street, Portland, ME, 04112
Tel: (207) 761-0660
Fax (207) 761-2913
www.salt.edu
email: salt@ime.net

Western Mountains & Lakes

• Poland Mining Camps — Poland

If you really want to learn about rocks and mineral collecting, the Poland Mining Camp is the place to stay. Everything (lodging, meals, mine fees and guide) is included in one price. Cost is based on choice of lodging and length of stay. Reservations are required and the season runs from Memorial Day to September 30. Owners Dudy and Mary Groves have exclusive collecting access to several mines.

Rt. 26 in Poland just before the junction with Rt. 11

PO Box 26, Poland, ME 04274.

(207) 998-2350

• The Celebration Barn — South Paris

If you're that special type of person who wants to know how to juggle, dance, perfect your mime routine and spin a better story, we have the place for you. Celebration Barn is just that — a barn set on 10 acres in the foothills of western Maine — where, since 1972, Tony Montanaro and his staff have provided workshops for mime, dance, improvisation, and storytelling. The Barn offers visiting performers, productions and instruction. Learn comedy, juggling, slapstick and much more.

190 Stock Farm Road

Tel: (207) 743-8452

Fax: (207) 743-3889

www.celebrationbarn.com

email: info@celebrationbarn.com

Midcoast

• The Morris Farm Trust — Wiscasset

A 50-acre working farm, agricultural education center and produce outlet. Open pastures and lush fields, a pond, barn, a small woodlot and farm buildings form an open outdoor classroom for people of all ages. The farm is dedicated to the belief that midcoast Maine farms are an important source of food as well as jobs, and an irreplaceable part of the landscape and social fabric of northern New England. Adult programs range from gardening and nutrition workshops, to seminars by advocates of sustainable agriculture and practitioners of traditional handcrafts, to farmer-to-farmer training and information exchanges. The farm also operates an organic farm apprentice program. All K-12 programs are tied to state academic achievement standards and provide hands-on, real-life educational

experience for children of all academic abilities.
PO Box 136, 156 Gardiner Road, Wiscasset, ME 04578
(207) 882-4080
www.morrisfarm.org
email: MorrisFarm@morrisfarm.org

• The Maine Photographic Workshops &
• The International Film & Television Workshops — Rockport
  This is the Maine campus of this internationally-renown organization, which offers 150 one- and two-week workshops and master classes, a four-week Filmmaking School and a one-year Professional Certificate Program in Filmmaking.
  Studies cover subjects including nature, wildlife, sports, fashion and landscape-photography, darkroom techniques, fine-art nude photography, photojournalism, portraiture, studio and advertising photography, architectural photography, digital photography, film and video photography and many others. Courses also in use of camera, alternate photographic processes, et al.
PO Box 200, 2 Central Street, Rockport, ME 04856
(207) 236-8581, 877-577-7700
www.theworkshops.com
email: info@theworkshops.com

D o w n   E a s t

• The Good Life Center — Harborside
  Located at the farm home of Scott Nearing (1883-1983) and Helen Knothe Nearing (1904-1995), the Good Life Center pursues their goal of cultivating the mind and spirit. Led by Rachel Glickman and Henry Zacchini and a staff of resident stewards who tend the farm and greet visitors. Offered are a varied series of seminars, workshops and talks on subjects ranging from Organic Gardening, Land Conservation and Wild Plants for Food and Medicine to Rediscovering our Musical Selves, Place & Poetry and Simple Living Around the World. All are led by experts from around the state and beyond — speakers like Jay Espy, President, Maine Coast Heritage Trust; Baron Wormser, Maine Poet Laureate; Gunnar Hansen, Environmental Journalist and Russell Libby, Executive Director, Maine Organic Farmers and Gardeners Association. Other past experts have included singer/composer Bernice Lewis; Chellie Pingree, former Maine Senate majority leader as well as farmer and business owner, and many others.
372 Harborside Road, Harborside, ME 04642
(207) 326-8211

www.goodlife.org
email: info@goodlife.org

• Haystack Mountain School of Crafts — Deer Isle
Founded in 1950, Haystack teaches fine craftsmanship, develops talent and creativity and investigates fine crafts' potential as visual art. Haystack visitors develop their skills and imagination and are encouraged to use their ideas to cultivate and nurture their creative spirit.

Workshops are open to adults; all skill-levels are welcome. Workshop subjects include blacksmithing, clay, fibers, glass, graphics, metals and wood. Studios are open 24 hours a day. Additional evening lectures, slide presentations by internationally-recognized faculty members, and performances by visiting artists and writers flavor the experience.
PO Box 518, Deer Isle, ME 04627
Tel: (207) 348-2306
Fax: (207) 358-2607
www.haystack-mtn.org/
 email: haystack@haystack-mtn.org

• The WoodenBoat School — Brooklin
You can learn to build your own boat here, from canoes and kayaks to dinghies and larger sailboats and workboats; restore old ones and learn the art of seamanship. Classes are held at the school's stunning 64-acre saltwater campus, where you can explore, cruise, practice and relax alongside skilled professional boatbuilders and sailors. Boat restoration is an essential part of the curriculum, too. Courses include Fundamentals of Boatbuilding, Wooden Boat Repair Methods, Marine Photography, Marine Carving, Coastwise Navigation, Canoe Repair and Restoration, Craft of Sail, Building the Chesapeake 17 Kayak, Windjamming Aboard the Lewis R. French and a host of other
Naskeag Road, PO Box 78, Brooklin, ME 04616
Tel: (207) 359-4651
Fax: (207) 359-8920
www.woodenboat.com
email: school@woodenboat.com

• Wendell Gilley Museum of Bird Carving — Southwest Harbor
This is your opportunity to learn how to carve a bird, or improve your bird- carving skills in a unique and beautiful museum setting. Summer and fall workshops are offered with the Gilley Museum Carver-in-Residence, Steven Valleau. Some sessions are especially for children, with beginner and intermediate

level adults welcome at all others. Learn how to carve and paint a merganser, yellow-bellied sapsucker, California quail or a white-winged scooter decoy. Workshops are from one day to 10 weeks with most lasting four days. Carving Club and special events scheduled during the winter months.
Wendell Gilley Museum
PO Box 254
Southwest Harbor, ME 04679
(207) 244-7555
www.acadia.net/gilley
email: gilleymu@acadia.net

• College of the Atlantic Family Nature Camp — Bar Harbor

This is a wonderful opportunity for the entire family to explore our environment in arguably one of the most beautiful areas on earth. The College of the Atlantic was founded three decades ago when it was becoming evident that conventional education was an inadequate preparation for citizenship in an increasingly complex and technical society. COA's founders created a pioneering institution dedicated to the interdisciplinary study of human ecology, a college in which students overcome narrow points of view and integrate knowledge across traditional academic lines. The College is located on 29 shorefront acres overlooking Frenchman Bay, adjacent to Acadia National Park.

There are six sessions (Sunday afternoon to Saturday morning) late June to early August. The program allows families (with children as young as 5) to learn about geology, take guided flora and fauna walks in Acadia National Park, ride a Whale Watch Boat, explore tidal pools, assemble a Minke Whale skeleton and learn a great deal about our ecology. The College provides housing, and parents and children share one or two bedrooms. These are accommodated in suites with other families.

COA provides three meals a day beginning with dinner Sunday evening and ending with a continental breakfast on Saturday. The kitchen always has "child-friendly" foods available. Family Nature Camp participants are required to participate in campus housing and meal program service.
College of the Atlantic Summer Programs
105 Eden Street, Bar Harbor, ME 04609
Tel: (800) 597-9500 or (207) 288-5015
Fax: (207) 288-4126
www.coa.edu/summer/famnaturecamp/index.html
email: summer@ecology.coa.edu

Kennebec & Moose River Valleys

• Maine Archaeological Society — Augusta

This may be your chance to find out what Maine was like a few hundred years ago, or perhaps 10,000 years ago. If prehistoric Indian campsites, colonial villages, forts or even shipwrecks interest you, this is where to begin. The MAS was founded in 1956 and is the statewide organization for anyone with an interest in Maine archaeology. Its membership includes amateur and professional archaeologists and people who just want to learn more about the subject. By joining the Society for as little as $8 to $15, you may have the opportunity to work on one of the numerous sites throughout the state.

PO Box 982 Augusta, ME 04332-0982

www.mainearchsociety.org

Lighthouses
(Maine's Sentinels of Hope)

Marshall Point Lighthouse, Port Clyde, by John Brough

The lighthouse and lightship appeal to the interests and better instinct of man because they are symbolic of never-ceasing watchfulness, of steadfast endurance in every exposure, of widespread helpfulness. The building and keeping of the lights is a picturesque and humanitarian work of the nation.

George R. Putnam
First Commissioner
Bureau of Lighthouses

* * *

Although it is virtually impossible to avoid tourists and crowds when visiting Maine's fabled lighthouses, no guide to Maine's attractions would be complete without their inclusion. We suggest planning your lighthouse visits with timing in mind — off days, off hours and even off-season are obviously key to enjoying them fully.

Lighthouses have been guiding mariners to safe harbor since ancient times. Other than fires occasionally lit on beaches and cliffs, and sometimes on the roofs of buildings, the first real lighthouse, most historians agree, was built around 300 B.C. on the island of Pharos at the head of the harbor in Alexandria, Egypt. It took 20 years to build, and stood over 500 feet high — a colossus included among the Seven Wonders of the Ancient World. It served for an astonishing thousand years, and remained intact for another 500 years after that until finally felled by an earthquake.

Since then, thousands of lighthouses have been erected around the world — well over 2,000 in the United States alone (only about 500 remain), including some 65 along the rocky shores and islands of Maine. For reasons that none can describe adequately, they all have had a captivating influence on those who have seen and visited them, not to mention the uncounted numbers who have been saved by them from certain disaster and, quite probably, death by drowning.

It is perhaps due to their noble purpose and the untarnished human goodness that they symbolize that our lighthouses are so universally revered. But there is, most certainly, more to it than that.

Lighthouses represent a unique connection between land and sea — between the safety of the one and the perils of the other. It's not difficult to imagine the joy and relief mariners must have experienced after months at sea with only the most rudimentary navigation aids when they saw that welcoming light from ashore. Nor is it a great leap to understand the appreciation seamen must feel to be guided safely past dangerous rocks and shoals by the night-piercing lights put there solely for that purpose. Lighthouses are, indeed, a reflection of one of the better aspects of human nature — man helping man with no conditions, no strings, no price.

There can be no other explanation for the remarkable dedication of those who tended the early lighthouses — crude oil-fired lamps that required nearly constant attention through almost unendurable weather conditions — day in and day out. The worse the conditions, in fact, the greater the need for the illuminating sentinels. From the many books filled with stories of the keepers' heroics comes a common theme: dedication, perseverance, selflessness.

One of the most frequently told is about Abbie Burgess, the 17-year-old daughter of the keeper of Matinicus Rock Light who saved her invalid mother and three younger sisters and then kept them alive when her father was trapped ashore for a month by severe storms in the winter of 1856. The fact that she never failed to keep the lighthouse lamp lit during the entire ordeal was considered heroism of the first magnitude.

She spent the rest of her life as a keeper at Matinicus Rock (marrying the son of her father's replacement) and, later, at White Head Light, some 20 miles closer to the mainland. She later wrote:

"It has always seemed to me that the light was part of myself.... Many nights I have watched the light [for] my part of the night, and then could not sleep the rest of the night thinking nervously what might happen should the light go out.

I wonder if the care of the lighthouse will follow my soul after it has left this worn out body!"

There are many such stories of lighthouse keepers and their families — of bravery, madness, ghosts, legends — the stuff of tales told and retold by a fascinated throng of lighthouse admirers. The lights and their accompanying foghorns are all automated now, no longer dependent on vigilant keepers.

The lighthouse structures themselves, of course, with their connection to the sea, their colorful history and their magnificent settings along coastal Maine, are quite enough to continue to awe and inspire present-day visitors.

Portland Head Light in Cape Elizabeth, Maine's first (authorized by none other than George Washington and built in 1791) is the state's most visited lighthouse. That it is in Cape Elizabeth, and not Portland, matters little.

Mt. Desert Rock Light, 20 miles out to sea, is among the most remote, and Boon Island Light is similarly perched on a small rock miles from the mainland. Matinicus Rock Light placed Abbie Burgess and her family some 25 miles from the nearest port. The peril of being precariously set so far out to sea is emphasized by records of huge boulders weighing up to 50 tons being thrown up by stormy seas onto the sites of both the Mt. Desert Rock and Boon Island lights. And at Boon Island, after many structures were repeatedly wrecked and washed into the sea by storms, all efforts to build a keeper's house were finally abandoned years ago by the Coast Guard.

You could easily start an argument in Maine about which lighthouse is the most beautiful, but the contenders would have to include Bass Harbor Light in Acadia National Park on Mt. Desert Island, Owls Head Light at the entrance to the harbor in Rockland, the Curtis Island Light in Camden Harbor, the candy-striped West Quoddy Head Light off Lubec and The Nubble (Cape Neddick Light), a photo of which was sent into outer space in 1977 aboard NASA's Voyager II spacecraft (an apparent effort to impress somebody out there). Pemaquid Point Light, perched high atop a shelf of granite, is also beautifully situated, as are the Ram Island and Burnt Island lights in the Boothbay Harbor region.

The Seguin Island Light, at the mouth of the Kennebec River, is the only Maine lighthouse equipped with a first-order Fresnel (pronounced Fre-nél) lens. It is also the highest above the water, and holds the record as the foggiest location of any light in America (with a nod to Point Reyes Light near San Francisco), once logging 2,734 hours of fog in a single year. The Boon Island light is the tallest structure at 133 feet.

Lighthouse lovers owe a debt to Winslow Lewis, who may well deserve the title of Father of American Lighthouses. He was commissioned in 1810 by Treasury Secretary Albert Gallatin to put his patented lenses in all of the nation's 49 lighthouses, and he built more than 100 more. He initially resisted Augustin

Fresnel's prism/refracting/magnifying lens concept, but later acceded to the Frenchman's superior design.

Just what it is about lighthouses that generates such ardor is hard to identify. They are, after all, just buildings with lights on top — not the tallest or most imposing, not the brightest or most penetrating beams. But they are monuments to the goodness of people who care about their fellow man. They are remnants of our nation's seafaring beginnings. And as has often been repeated, lighthouses are to America what castles are to Europe.

*   *   *

Lighthouses are not just romantic, lonely sentinels against a dark and evil sea. They're symbols of hope — and defiance.

> Wayne C. Wheeler
> President
> U.S. Lighthouse Society

From south to north...

• Whaleback Light
Portsmouth Harbor. Built in 1831, it stands 59 feet above sea level.

• Boon Island Light
Six miles off Cape Neddick. Built in 1880, it is Maine's tallest lighthouse at 133 feet.

• Cape Neddick Light (The Nubble)
Arguably Maine's most photographed lighthouse (a photo of it was sent into outer space in 1977 aboard NASA's Voyager II spacecraft), The Nubble was built in 1879, and stands 88 feet above sea level on a tiny islet a few yards off Cape Neddick in York. Best viewed from Sohier Park in York.

• Goat Island Light
Built in 1833 on Goat Island off Kennebunkport, it is 38 feet above the water.

• Wood Island Light
Built in 1808 just offshore from Biddeford Pool, and said to be haunted, it is also 38 feet above sea level.

• Cape Elizabeth Light
Actually two lights, built in 1828, although one was permanently turned off in 1924. The remaining light is the most powerful of New England lights, and stands 129 feet above sea level.

• Portland Head Light
Maine's oldest, commissioned by George Washington, and arguably the most visited (and, therefore, crowded). It stands 101 feet above the water in Cape Elizabeth (not Portland).

• Spring Point Ledge
This one is in Portland. It stands 54 feet above sea level, and was built in 1855.

• Bug Light
Also known as the Portland Breakwater Light (although located in South Portland), built in 1855, inactive since 1942.

• Ram Island Ledge Light
Completely surrounded by water at high tide, built in 1905 offshore from Portland, 77 feet above the water.

• Halfway Rock Light
The "halfway" refers to its location between Cape Elizabeth and Cape Small, 11 miles northeast of Portland. 77 feet above sea level.

• Doubling Point Light
Located in Bath, built in 1898, 25 feet above the sea.

• Kennebec River Range Lights
Two lights near Bath, one 18 feet above the water and the other 33 feet, help ships position themselves in the middle of the river channel. Built in 1908.

• Squirrel Point Light
Built in 1898 on Arrowsic Island, 23 feet above sea level.

• Perkins Island Light
Now "endangered," the light was built in 1898 on the eastern side of the Kennebec River, 41 feet above the water.

• Pond Island Light
Built in 1821, also on the east side of the Kennebec, but on an island 900 yards off Popham Beach. 52 feet above the water.

• Seguin Island Light
Maine's second oldest light, built in 1795, also by President Washington's order, and the state's only first-order Fresnel lens. The 53-foot granite tower is perched atop a 153-foot high island bluff two miles off Popham Beach. This light's height and power make it visible far out to sea.

• Hendrick's Head Light
Built in 1829 on Southport Island at the mouth of the Sheepscot River. 43 feet above sea level. Site of a dramatic historical rescue, and supposedly haunted, as well.

• The Cuckolds Light
Built in 1907, 59 feet above sea level, about a mile off Southport Island.

• Burnt Island Light
Built in 1821 at the entrance to Boothbay Harbor, 61 feet above the water.

• Ram Island Light
On the other side of the Boothbay Harbor entrance, 36 feet above the sea, built in 1833.

• Pemaquid Point Light
Built in 1827 and rebuilt in 1857, commissioned by John Quincy Adams, 79 feet.

• Franklin Island Light
Built in 1855, five miles off Friendship in Muscongus Bay, 57 feet above sea level.

• Monhegan Island Light
Built in 1824 nine miles off Rockland, often the first sighting of trans-Atlantic voyagers, 178 feet above sea level.

• Marshall Point Light
Built in 1832 and rebuilt in 1857, located at the entrance to Port Clyde Harbor, 30 feet above the water.

• Tenants Harbor Light
Built in 1857 just offshore from the Southern Island and the harbor. Now inactive, it is owned and maintained by the Wyeth family.

• Whitehead Light
Built in 1807 by order of Thomas Jefferson, rebuilt in 1852. Marks the entrance to Muscle Ridge Channel on a small island near Tenants Harbor, 75 feet above the sea.

• Owls Head Light
Built in 1825 near Rockland in Penobscot Bay, Only 20 feet tall, but 100 feet above sea level.

• Rockland Breakwater Light
Built in 1888, rebuilt in 1902, at the end of a stone jetty, standing 39 feet above sea level.

• Matinicus Rock Light
Originally twin towers built in 1827, rebuilt in 1848 and 1857, on isolated rock five miles off Matinicus Island, 25 miles out to sea from Rockland. 90 feet above sea level, and the light where Abbie Burgess gained hero status in the winter of 1856.

• Two Bush Island Light
Built in 1897 opposite Owls Head Light on Penobscot Bay, 65 feet above the water.

• Indian Island Light
Built in 1851, but not operational until 1875, at the eastern end of Rockport Harbor off Beauchamp Point. Privately owned, inactive since 1933.

• Heron Neck Light
Built in 1854 on the southern tip of Green Island southwest of Carver's Harbor on Vinalhaven, marking the entrance to Hurricane Sound, 92 feet above the water.

• Brown's Head Light
Built in 1832 and rebuilt in 1857 on the northwest point of Vinalhaven marking the end of the Fox Island thoroughfare, 39 feet above the water.

• Curtis Island Light
Built in 1836 on the south side of the entrance to Camden Harbor, 52 feet above sea level.

• Goose Rocks Light
Built in 1890 on ledge between Vinalhaven and North Haven islands, 51 feet above the water.

• Grindle Point Light
Built in 1851 on Islesboro Island at the entrance to Gilkey Harbor. Solar powered, the light stands 39 feet above the sea.

• Fort Point Light
Built in 1836 by order of President Andrew Jackson, rebuilt in 1857, at the mouth of the Penobscot River in Stockton Springs, 88 feet above the water.

• Dice Head Light
Built in 1829 and rebuilt in 1858 and 1937 in Castine. No longer active.

• Eagle Island Light
Built in 1839 and rebuilt in 1858 between Deer Isle and North Haven in Penobscot Bay, 106 feet above the water.

• Pumpkin Island Light
Built in 1854 at the northern end of Eggemoggin Reach off Little Deer Isle. No longer active, privately owned.

• Blue Hill Bay Light
Built in 1856 on Green Island. No longer active.

• Mark Island Light
Built in 1857 on the west end of Mark Island on the approach to Deer Isle, 52 feet above sea level.

• Isle au Haut Light
Built in 1907 on Robinson Point in Stonington near Kimball Island, 48 feet above the water.

• Saddleback Ledge Light
Built in 1839, 48 feet above sea level.

• Burnt Coat Harbor Light
Built in 1972 at Hockmock Head on Swans Island, 75 feet above the water.

• Bass Harbor Head Light
Built in 1858 on Mount Desert Island marking the entrance to Blue Hill Bay and Bass Harbor, 56 feet above the water.

• Bear Island Light
Built in 1839, rebuilt in 1889 at the entrance to the harbor at Mount Desert Island, 100 feet above sea level.

• Baker Island Light
Built in 1828 by order of John Quincy Adams, rebuilt in 1855, at the entrance to Frenchman's Bay, 105 feet above the water.

• Mount Desert Rock Light
Built in 1830 on a tiny island 25 miles off Mount Desert Island, 75 feet above the sea.

• Great Duck Island Light
Built in 1890 six miles southeast of Bass Harbor, 67 feet above the water.

• Egg Rock Light
Built in 1875 at the entrance to Frenchman's Bay, 64 feet above sea level.

• Prospect Harbor Light
Built in 1850, rebuilt in 1891 on the east side of the inner harbor, 42 feet above the water.

• Winter Harbor Light
Built in 1856 on Mark Island on Frenchman's Bay. No longer active, privately-owned.

• Narraguagus Island Light
Built in 1853 on Pond Island in Narraguagus Bay. No longer active.

• Petit Manan Light
Built in 1817, rebuilt in 1855, the second tallest lighthouse in Maine at 119 feet high, on a small island off Petit Manan Point in South Milbridge.

• Nash Island Light
Built in 1838, rebuilt in 1872, at the entrance to Pleasant Bay. No longer active.

• Moose Peak Light
Built in 1827, rebuilt in 1887, on the east side of Mistake Island south of Jonesboro, 72 feet above sea level.

• Libby Island Light
Built in 1817, rebuilt in 1824, on the southern tip of Libby Island at the entrance to Machias Bay, 91 feet above the water.

• Little River Light
Built in 1847, rebuilt in 1876, at the entrance to Cutler Harbor. Long inactive, this light was lovingly restored in 2001 by volunteers and contributors under the auspices of the American Lighthouse Association.

• West Quoddy Light
Built in Whiting in 1807 by order of President Thomas Jefferson. This distinctive red-and-white striped light on Passamoquoddy Bay overlooks the Bay of Fundy, 83 feet above sea level. Its colorful striping follows the Canadian custom, thought to make such structures easier to see from offshore in fog and against a snowy background.

• Lubec Channel Light
Built in 1890 on the west side of the channel. Often referred to as the "Spark Plug," 53 feet above sea level.

• Whitlock's Mill Light
Built in 1892 on the bank of the St. Croix River in Calais, 32 feet above the water.

Select Lodging

The Blair Hill Inn, Greenville, by Dick Balkite

You won't have any trouble finding the many hotels and motels that dot the landscape of Maine. More difficult is finding truly enjoyable accommodations off the beaten track, away from the madding crowds, yet situated to give you a base of operations from which to enjoy the great state of Maine.

We carefully selected the best from among the many hundreds of inns, lodges and B&Bs to provide the discriminating visitor a pleasant, even memorable stay, be it for a night, a weekend or even longer.

Southern Coastal

Inns & Lodges

• Dockside Guest Quarters — York Harbor
Tucked out of the way on a peninsula jutting into the middle of beautiful York Harbor, all 19 rooms boast antique furnishings, marine art and stunning water views. On-site river cruises, boat rentals, bikes, lawn games; fishing, sailing, lobsterboat rides and golf nearby, as is historic York Village. Complete dining facilities with water views from every table.
Harris Island Road, York, ME 03909
Take Route 1A through York; turn right on Route 103, take first left immediately after bridge, follow to end. (207) 363-2868, 1-800-270-1977
email: info@docksidegq.com

• The Viewpoint — York Beach
Although located in a popular tourist destination, this luxurious inn is a true

get-away oasis offering one-, two- and three-bedroom suites, all extravagantly-equipped (fireplace, full kitchen, VCR, CD stereo, private deck) with unparalleled views of the rocky coast and The Nubble Lighthouse just off shore. Beautiful, uncommonly quiet and relaxing. Daily, weekly and weekend — plus winter-getaway weekend packages.

Take Route 1A through York and past Long Sands Beach, take right on Nubble Road and continue past entrance to Sohier Park. 229 Nubble Road, York Beach, ME 03910
(207) 363-2661
www.viewpoint-maine.com
email: viewpnt@aol.com

• Cape Arundel Inn — Kennebunkport
If this place offered nothing more than its location, it would be enough — right on the ocean (near Walker's Point, the Bush family's peninsula estate). Sit on the front porch and search the horizon for ocean-going vessels. Breakfast is included, but the dining room is open to the public for dinner, which is very special indeed. Rooms are well appointed, comfortably elegant.
Ocean Avenue, Kennebunkport, ME 04046
(207) 967-2125

• The Tides Inn By-The-Sea — Goose Rocks Beach
Century-old Victorian inn with ocean views and direct beach access, 22 rooms, each with different decor (and prices), complete dining facilities. Ocean-front cottage-suites by the week. Golf, tennis, fishing, museums, whale-watching and antique shopping nearby. Prior guests include Teddy Roosevelt and Sir Arthur Conan Doyle (and Emma, a friendly ghost who so enjoyed her stay that she refuses to leave).

Take Route 9 north from Kennebunkport to The Clock Farm; turn right on to Dyke Road. Turn left at end and continue one-half mile to inn.
252 Goose Rocks Beach, ME 04046
(207) 967-3757
www.tidesinnbythesea.com

Bed & Breakfasts

• Inn at Harmon Park — York Harbor
If it's breakfast you savor, this is your place. A comfortable, warm atmosphere throughout, within easy walking distance to the York River, the York Harbor Beach and dramatic Mason Estate Park on the bluff overlooking the ocean. But

don't sleep in or you'll miss one of the most unique, interesting and delicious breakfasts you're apt to find anywhere.

Take Route 1A off Route 1 in York and continue into York Harbor to the intersection of York Street (Route 1A) and Harmon Park.
PO Box 495, York Harbor, ME 03911
(207) 363-2031
www.yorkme.org/inns/harmonpark.html
email: santal@gwi.net

• Edwards' Harborside Inn — York Harbor
Spectacular views of York Harbor and York Harbor Beach greet guests at this stately house, including when they're enjoying breakfast in the sun porch. The York Suite has water views on three sides — even a water view from the hot tub. Tennis, golf, boating, fishing, shopping are all within minutes, but you might prefer just to sit in a lawn chair and enjoy the scenery.

Take Route 1A from Route 1, continue through harbor area and turn right onto Stage Neck.
PO Box 866, York Harbor, ME 03911
(207) 363-3037

• Captain Lord Mansion — Kennebunkport
Built in 1814, this is a splendid example of a Federal mansion. It has 16 beautifully-decorated rooms, all but one with a gas fireplace, all with four-poster or canopy beds. One, the Merchant Captain's Suite, has what may be the largest bathroom of any Maine B&B. You can view the town and the sea from the widow's walk three stories up. The place is elegant (and expensive), but breakfast is informal. Phebe's Fantasy, a separate building, offers four more rooms with fireplaces.

Corner of Green and Pleasant streets, Kennebunkport.
PO Box 800, Kennebunk, ME 04046
(207) 967-3141

• 1802 House — Kennebunkport
Situated along the 15th fairway of the Cape Arundel Golf club, this quiet, six-room historic B&B was built almost 200 years ago, but renovated in 1999. Each room has luxury amenities such as a CD player, a TV/VCR, a fireplace and a whirlpool tub.

Take Route 35 to Kennebunk, turn left on Route 9 to Kennebunkport.
15 Locke St., Kennebunkport, ME 04046
(207) 967-5632, 1-800-932-5632

Greater Portland

Inns & Lodges

• The Danforth — Portland
If you must stay in Portland, this is one of the places that offer gracious comfort — an 1821 inn on Tyng Street overlooking the waterfront area. Rooms boast working fireplaces, and breakfast is special. Other attractions: billiard room, library, cupola up top for great sunrises and sunsets.
A163 Danforth Street, Portland, ME 04104
(207) 879-8755, 1-800-991-6557
www.danforthmaine.com
email: danforth@maine.rr.com

• Pomegranate Inn — Portland
Another special inn, this one on the beautiful western promenade historical residential district. If you can get the carriage house — upstairs suite, guestroom down with private terrace — go for it. And enjoy the complimentary wine and tea when you arrive.
49 Neal Street, Portland, ME 04102
(207) 773-4426, 1-800-356-0408
www.pomegranateinn.com

• Portland Regency — Portland
One of only two large hotels (95 rooms) you'll find in this book — but as noted, if you must stay in Portland.... A classic historic hotel in the grand tradition in what was once an old armory, now elegant and comfortable. Full services, including meeting facilities, a health club, restaurant and lounge.
20 Milk Street, Portland, ME 04101
(207) 774-4200, 1-800-727-3436
www.theregency.com
email: public@theregency.com

• Black Point Inn Resort — Prouts Neck
One of the best places to stay in Portland because it's really not in Portland. A classic 1878 summer hotel with 80 rooms (this is the other one), indoor and outdoor pools, two whirlpools, a sauna. Guests are welcomed at the Prouts Neck Country Club golf course and 14-court tennis complex nearby, and may even moor boats at the local yacht club. Rooms offer southern coast and open-ocean views. Prouts Neck bird sanctuary is nearby.

Take Route 114 off I-95 through Scarborough; turn right onto Route 207.
Prouts Neck, ME 04074
(207) 883-2500, 1-800-258-0003

• Diamond Cove — Diamond Island, Casco Bay
     Resort built on island site of old Fort McKinley, with beach, heated pool, tennis, hiking, biking, fishing. Mooring facilities available (the only way to get there is by boat or ferry). Diamond's Edge serves up a varied menu. Your own little corner of the planet with a great Sunday brunch thrown in for good measure.
PO Box 3572, Portland, ME 04104
(207) 772-2992

Bed & Breakfasts

• Quaker Tavern — Falmouth
     This ca. 1780 Federal house, a National Historic Landmark surrounded by 15 acres of farm and forest (yet within eight miles of the Portland Jetport and Portland Harbor), features fireplaces in every room, feather beds and candlelight breakfasts.
     377 Gray Road, Route 26 North, Falmouth, ME 04105
(207) 797-5540
www.bbme-mex.com/quakertavern/home/html
email: quakerbb@aol.com

Western Mountains & Lakes

Inns & Lodges

• Oxford House Inn — Fryeburg
     Comfortable, well-appointed accommodations with elegant dining just downstairs. Picturesque setting (with great views of the nearby White Mountains); small mountain village atmosphere, yet within striking distance of outlet malls in North Conway, just over the border in New Hampshire. On Main Street in Fryeburg, home of the Fryeburg Fair.
     105 Main Street, Fryeburg, ME 04037
(207) 935-3442 or 1-800-261-7206
www.oxfordhouseinn.com
email: innkeeper@oxfordhouseinn.com

• Admiral Peary House — Fryeburg

Once the home of the famous explorer, the mountain inn offers tennis (on a well-kept private clay court), hiking, canoeing and swimming in the Saco River, boat rides on Kezar Lake, an outdoor whirlpool, perennial gardens and six comfortable rooms. Only 15 minutes — but a seeming ocean — away from the super-shopping in North Conway. A billiard room is a special offering.

Route 5 or Route 302 to Fryeburg. Take Elm Street directly across from the Post Office.

9 Elm St., Fryeburg, ME 04037

(207) 935-3365, 1-800-237-8080

www.mountwashingtonvalley.com/admiralpearyhouse

email: admpeary@nxi.com

• Pleasant Point Inn on Kezar Lake

A pine-forest-surrounded shorefront inn on Kezar Lake, which offers boating, swimming and extraordinary fishing (salmon, trout, bass). Two tennis courts on site, golf nearby. Free canoes for use on the lake, which National Geographic calls one of the three most beautiful on the planet (and Stephen King, a local, agrees). Boat rentals. Six rooms, each with lake views, all recently (1994) refurbished.

Pleasant Point Rd., Center Lovell, ME 04051

(207) 925-3008

email: ppi@pleasantpoint.com

• Quisisana — Kezar Lake

The spot for music lovers. Each evening features a concert performed by music students from leading music schools, who have been coming here to play and enjoy since 1917. Besides the 75 guest rooms, there are small cottages in the woods and along the lake shore. Croquet, tennis, swimming, water-skiing, boating, fishing (guides available). Good food, too.

Kezar Lake, Center Lovell, ME 04016

(207) 925-3500

• Inn on Winter's Hill — Kingfield

A Classic Georgian Revival mansion designed by the Stanley brothers, better-known for their steamer cars, in 1895 and fully restored in 1990. Hike the Appalachian Trail or climb a mountain, bike (on-road and off-), fish the Carrabassett River and nearby lakes. Indoor and outdoor swimming, pool table, bar and full dining facilities. Clay tennis court, hot tub.

Take Route 27 north from Augusta.
RR#1 Box 1272, Winter Hill Rd., Kingfield, ME 04947
1-800-233-9687

Bed & Breakfasts

• Acres of Austria — Fryeburg
Located on 65 pine-forested acres, this retreat offers a touch of the old country, with menu favorites such as Jaegerschnitzel, Schweinsbraten and Kas'nockn', special Austrian holiday celebrations and even Carombol on the billiard table. Canoeing on the Saco River, hiking amid wildlife and unspoiled flora, horseback-riding, golf, tennis, concerts, theater and more all nearby, as is outlet shopping in North Conway just across the border in New Hampshire.
Take Route 5 north from intersection of Route 302 for seven miles.
Route 5, Fryeburg, ME 04037
(207) 925-6547, 1-800-988-4391
www.acresofaustria.com
email: info@acresofaustria.com

Midcoast

Inns & Lodges

• The Lawnmeer Inn — Southport Island
Just one swing bridge and a few miles away, but far from the bustling Boothbay area, this waterfront inn has been welcoming visitors for over a century. The picturesque Pemaquid Point Lighthouse is nearby, and quaint fishing villages are within view from your private balcony or deck. Complete dining facilities. Fishing, boating, island ferries nearby. The famous Burnt Island and "The Cuckolds" lighthouses are also nearby.
Take Route 27 east from Route 1 across the bridge from Wiscasset through Boothbay Harbor; continue over bridge to Southport Island.
PO Box 505, West Boothbay Harbor, ME 04575
(207) 633-2544, 1-800-633-SMILE (7645)

• Ocean Point Inn — Southport Island
Your choice of a cottage or a guest room in this waterside inn on Linekin Bay six miles from Boothbay Harbor. Full dining facilities (with lobster, crab cakes and fresh salmon specialties daily), swimming pool, some kitchenettes. Fishing, golf and tennis nearby. Deep-sea fishing, sailing charters and sightseeing cruises

as well as biking, kayaking and rowing also available. Day-trips to islands, lighthouses.

Take Route 27 east from Route 1 across the bridge from Wiscasset toward Boothbay Harbor; turn left onto Route 96 and continue to Middle Road on Linekin Neck. Take right off Middle Road onto Shore Road.
Shore Road, East Boothbay, ME 04544
(207) 633-4200, 1-800-552-5554
www.oceanpointinn.com
email: opi@oceanpointinn.com

• Newagen Seaside Inn — Southport Island
Set on 85 acres at the seaward tip of the island, six miles "out to sea" from Boothbay Harbor, this inn is a full-service resort, with tennis, rowboats, fresh-water and salt-water swimming pools and complete dining facilities. Golf, sail- and power-boat rentals, horseback riding, galleries, museums and charter boats are available nearby. Most rooms have ocean views. "The Cuckolds" Lighthouse is also nearby.

Follow Route 27 through Boothbay Harbor and continue to Newagen at the tip of the island.
Route 27, Southport Island, Cape Newagen, ME 04576
1-800-654-5242
www.newagenseasideinn.com
email: innkeepers@newageninn.com

• Squire Tarbox Inn — Westport Island
Arguably the quietest spot in the midcoast region, this country inn features a 1763 farmhouse and converted barn. While elegant, it is also a working farm, complete with animals, et al. A house rowboat awaits at the saltwater inlet, and you can both witness the making of goat cheese in the barn and sample it at cocktail time in the parlor. All rooms have private baths and king or queen beds. Complete dining facilities.
1181 Westport Island Rd., Wiscasset, ME 04578
(207) 882-7693

• The Newcastle Inn — Newcastle
Romantic 1850 country inn (renovated in 1990) with views of the Damariscotta River boat harbor and beautiful perennial gardens. Country-French cuisine. 14 rooms feature king or queen canopy or four-poster beds, fireplaces, Jacuzzis. Winner of Waverly/Country Inns Magazine Room of the Year

award. Central midcoast location.

Take right on River Road off Route 1 approx. 10 miles after crossing
Sheepscot River Bridge in Wiscasset.
60 River Road, Newcastle, ME 04553
(207) 563-5685, 1-800-832-8669

• The East Wind Inn — Tenants Harbor
The Main Inn, Meeting House and Wheeler Cottage offer a variety of
accommodations, all restored, antique-filled and with harbor views. Wrap-around
porches, complete dining facilities, plus wharf chandlery with casual dining on
the water. Nearby Port Clyde offers Marshall Point Lighthouse, and connects
you to island ferries. Sailing, swimming, golf, tennis, hiking, kayaking and
biking available.

Take Route 131 off Route 1 just east of Thomaston 9.5 miles; turn left at Post
Office in Tenant's Harbor.
Mechanic St., Tenants Harbor, ME 04860
(207) 372-6366, 1-800-241-VIEW
www.eastwindinn.com
email: info@eastwindinn.com

• Bradley Inn — New Harbor
This restored 1898 inn, renovated in 1990, is a beautiful three-story, 16-room
oasis in a picturesque garden setting. It is located almost at the end of the
Pemaquid peninsula across the Damariscotta and St. Johns rivers from Boothbay
Harbor. The famed Fort William Henry and Pemaquid Lighthouse are nearby, as
are Pemaquid Beach and the Rachel Carson Salt Pond Reserve.

Route 1 to Route 1A to Damariscotta. Take right onto Route 130 through
Bristol to New Harbor.
3063 Bristol Road
New Harbor, ME 04554
(207) 677-2105, 1-800-492-5560

• Berry Manor Inn — Rockland
Graciously-restored Victorian mansion (eight guest rooms in three-story
house) in quiet residential neighborhood. Beautifully-decorated rooms feature
whirlpool tubs, working fireplaces, fluffy robes, phones with dataports. Walk to
Rockland's busy working harbor. Access to whale-watching trips, windjammer
cruises, Owls Head and Rockland Breakwater lighthouses, the Farnsworth
Museum. Home to Schooner and Lobster festivals, nearby Rockport Opera
House and Friendship Sloop Days.

Route 1 to Rockland.
81 Talbot Ave.
Rockland, ME 04841
(207) 596-7696, 1-800-774-5692
email: brymnrin@midcoast.com

• Mount Battie Lodge — Lincolnville Beach
Choose swimming on the beach or in a fresh-water lake, then relax among the woods, decks, gazebo and gardens that surround this rustic inn. Connecting rooms are ideal for families, or even when visiting the area with friends. Breakfasts are a major meal here, and access to the Camden area is only a few miles — and another world — away.
North on Route 1 from Camden.
Coastal Route 1, RR#3, Box 570, Lincolnville Beach, ME 04849
(207) 236-3870, 1-800-224-3870
www.acadia.net/mtbattie
email: mtbattie@acadia.net

• Blue Harbor House — Camden
A restored 1810 cape featuring country antiques and hand-fashioned quilts. Several rooms have canopy beds, fireplaces and whirlpool baths or antique soaking tubs. Breakfast offers stuffed French toast, chocolate breakfast tacos and blueberry pancakes. Dinners are also fine — including a Lobster Lover's Special, which comes with a two-hour sailing excursion on Penobscot Bay.
67 Elm St., Camden, ME 04843
(207) 236-3196, 1-800-248-3196
email: balidog@midcoast.com

• Belmont Inn — Camden
Nicely restored Edwardian gem on a quiet side street, with beautifully-appointed rooms, a great breakfast and a dining room presided over by a master chef, offering "unpretentious elegance and innovative cuisine." Close to everything.
6 Belmont Street, Camden, ME 04843
(207) 236-8053 or 1-800-238-8053
www.thebelmontinn.com

• Belfast Bay Meadows Inn by the Sea — Belfast
Seaside 1890 Country Inn, renovated in 1995, on 17 acres with forest paths, gardens and views of Penobscot Bay. Hiking, horseback riding, golf, tennis ashore; sailing, kayaking, schooner rides, boat rentals and charters on the bay. A plus: the

Moosehead Lake RR and Voyager tour boat.
192 Northport Ave., Belfast, ME 04915
(207) 338-5715, 1-800-335-2370

• Watchtide by the Sea — Searsport
Beautifully restored 1794 gem — listed in the National Register of Historic Places — with four pleasant rooms and a 60-foot sun porch overlooking Penobscot Bay and a bird and wildlife sanctuary. Ocean-view room offers a skylight and a double whirlpool. Walk to Moosepoint State Park beach. Guests get discount at Angels to Antiques gift shop on premises.
Route 1 between Belfast and Orland.
190 Main St., Searsport, ME 04794
(207) 548-6575, 1-800-698-6575
www.watchtide.com
email: stay@watchtide.com

Bed & Breakfasts

• Linekin Bay — East Boothbay
Historic 1878 home overlooking Linekin Bay with four spacious guest rooms, three with ocean views and two with fireplaces. Breakfasts include French toast a l'orange, home-made quiche, sour-cream waffles, more. Close (but not too close) to Boothbay Harbor attractions, shopping, dining. Deep-sea fishing, sailing cruises, whale-watching trips, lighthouses and Linekin Preserve all nearby.
771 Ocean Point Road, East Boothbay, ME 04544
(207) 633-9900
www.linekinbaybb.com
email: info@linekinbaybb.com

• The Five Gables — East Boothbay
Reminiscent of an old Victorian Maine hotel — this 100-year-plus inn, recently restored, offers 15 rooms (five with fireplaces) and a huge porch overlooking Linekin Bay. Nearby whale-watching trips, windjammer cruises, lighthouses, and easy access to the Boothbay Harbor area.
Take Route 27 east from Route 1 across the bridge from Wiscasset toward Boothbay Harbor; turn left onto Route 96 and continue to East Boothbay.
PO Box 335, East Boothbay, ME 04544
(207) 633-4551, 1-800-451-5048
email: info@fivegablesinn.com

• Harbor Hill — Friendship

Century-old farmhouse overlooking the harbor and islands of Friendship, a midcoast fishing village. Three guest suites and a two-bedroom apartment. Three-course Scandinavian-style or traditional Maine breakfast. Nearby attractions include the Farnsworth Museum in Rockland, also the home of Schooner and Lobster festivals, the Rockport Opera House and Friendship Sloop Days.

Take first right after "Welcome to Waldoboro" sign on Route 1. Take another right onto Route 220 in Waldoboro Center; go 10 miles to Friendship. Turn right again at library and then a left after the Post Office onto Town Landing Road.
5 Harbor Hill Lane, Friendship, ME 04547
(207) 832-6646

• Harbor View — Newcastle

Restored New England cape on a knoll above Newcastle and Damariscotta overlooking the river. Innkeeper/chef makes breakfast truly special. All guest rooms are large with tiled baths, roomy sitting areas, cable and phones. Several offer king- and queen-sized beds, private decks and fireplaces. Nearby whale-watching and puffin boat tours, island ferries, the Pemaquid fort and lighthouse, Popham Beach, Fort Baldwin and Reid State Park.

Route 1 north to Newcastle/Damariscotta "Exit for Business" Route 1 north. After .2 miles, turn into the first driveway on your left as you leave the exit ramp.
PO Box 791, Newcastle, ME 04553
(207) 563-2900

• The Inn at Sunrise Point — Lincolnville Beach

A luxury B&B on a luxurious, four-acre ocean-front estate. Cottages with great water views, some with whirlpool tubs and fireplaces, all with king and queen beds. Three rooms in the main house have fireplaces and water views. TVs and VCRs are in all rooms.
PO Box 1344, Lincolnville, ME 04849
(207) 236-7716, 1-800-435-6278

• Edgecombe-Coles House — Camden

Near Camden Harbor, but only a mile from Camden Hills State Park, sits this warm home listed on the National Register of Historic Places. Breakfast is hearty, and the views overlooking both mountains on one side and Penobscot Bay on the other are worth the visit. Use of bicycles is free.
RR#1 Box 3010, 64 High Street, Camden, ME 04843
(207) 236-2336, 1-800-528-2336
email: edgcmcol@midcoast.com

• Blackberry Inn — Camden
Remarkably restored 1850 Victorian with parlors, parquet floors, tin ceilings and ornate plaster moldings — the only home in Maine featured in "Daughters of Painted Ladies: America's Resplendent Victorians." Breakfasts fulfill the gourmet promise, whether served in the beautiful dining room or in the courtyard. Rooms offer fireplaces, whirlpool and clawfoot tubs and more.
82 Elm St., Camden, ME 04843
(207) 236-6060, 1-800-388-6000
email: blkberry@midcoast.com

• Dark Harbor House — Islesboro
The island's only hostelry, yet one of the Midcoast's best, is situated atop a hill and among landscaped gardens. All 10 rooms have private baths. Common areas are delightful. If the master suite is available, it's worth the extra money for the sun porch, fireplace and canopied queen-size bed. Antiques enhance the whole place. Dinner is special, and they'll prepare a picnic basket for your day trips around the island.
Box 185, Main Road, Dark Harbor, Islesboro, ME 04848
(207) 734-6669

• The White House — Belfast
This Greek Revival mansion is itself an attraction, registered in the National Register of Historic Places, with Italian marble fireplaces, plaster ceiling medallions, cornices and antique furnishings. Located at the foot of the square at the beginning of the Belfast historic district. Central location provides easy access to area attractions.
1 Church St., Belfast, ME 04915
(207) 338-1901, 1-888-290-1901
email: whitehouse@mainebb.com

• The Alden House — Belfast
Another example of beautiful architecture reminiscent of an earlier Maine era. Four working fireplaces, marble mantels, hand-carved cherry banister leading to seven bedrooms featuring featherbeds, antique decor and one — the Hiram Alden room — with a unique hand-carved cherry floor-to-ceiling mantel. Built in 1840, renovated in 1997.
63 Church St., Belfast, ME 04915
(207) 338-2151

• The Homeport Inn — Searsport

A fine example of a New England sea captain's mansion handsomely appointed with antiques and family heirlooms. Location amid seacoast towns and equidistant between Bangor and Bar Harbor, this B&B offers a good place to access major attractions while avoiding crowds and enjoying small-town Maine coast hospitality.

Route 1 midway between Belfast and Stockton Springs.

PO Box 647 Route 1, Searsport, ME 04794

(207) 548-2259

email: hportinn@acadia.net

Down East

Inns & Lodges

• Oceanside Meadows Inn — Prospect Harbor

A sea captain's home on 200 acres at the head of Sand Cove in picturesque Prospect Harbor with a sandy beach and spectacular views. Seven attractive, comfortable rooms plus several multi-room suites with full kitchens. Relax while hiking, bird-watching, sailing, kayaking and canoeing, biking and, if you're hardy enough, swimming.

Take ME 195 (Corea Road) off Route 1.

PO Box 90, Prospect Harbor, ME 04669

(207) 963-5557

http://travelassist.com/reg/me623.html

email: oceaninn@oceaninn.com

• The Brooklin Inn — Brooklin

A small inn in a small, beautiful coastal community (but which is home to WoodenBoat magazine and its associated boat-building school). Its Eggemoggin Reach location is central to Castine, Blue Hill and Stonington. Irish Pub is open daily, with access to an extensive wine cellar. Boating, whale-watching, kayaking, biking, relaxing in a quiet, out-of-the-way locale.

Take Route 15 from Route 1 east of Bucksport, then follow Route 175 to Brooklin.

Route 175, Brooklin, ME 04616

(207) 359-2777

www.brooklininn.com

email: chipandgail@brooklininn.com

• The Castine Inn — Castine

Harbor views here must compete with beautiful gardens. Three two-room suites offer special accommodations. The dining menu is superb — from Penobscot Bay crab cakes to roasted quail with a morel torte to raspberry creme brulee with a morier/fourme d'ambert/banon/crottin thrown in for good measure. Boating, sailing, whale-watching, golf, tennis, swimming with Acadia National Park nearby.

PO Box 41, Castine, ME 04421
(207) 326-4365
www.castineinn.com
email: relax@castineinn.com

• Kingsleigh Inn 1904 — Southwest Harbor

This little fishing village on the "quiet side" of Mt. Desert Island offers access to all that Bar Harbor has to offer without the busloads of tourists. Many rooms have beautiful harbor views, one in particular — the Turret Suite — has three secluded rooms and a working fireplace. Afternoon tea is a special occasion at the inn.

Route 3 to Mt. Desert Island. Bear right after bridge on Route 102 and continue to Southwest Harbor.

373 Main St., Southwest Harbor, ME 04679
(207) 244-7691
www.kingsleighinn.com

• The Moorings — Southwest Harbor

Located right on the shore of Somes Sound, this inn offers single rooms, doubles, suites and individual cottages, all with views of the water and the mountains of Acadia National Park. Right next to Hinckley Yacht.

Route 3 to Mt. Desert Island. Bear right after bridge on Route 102 and continue to Southwest Harbor.

P.O. Box 744, Southwest Harbor, ME 04679
(207) 244-5523
www.mooringsinn.com
email: storey@acadia.net

• The Ledgelawn Inn — Bar Harbor

This relaxed but breathtakingly beautiful inn, although in the heart of Bar Harbor, is reminiscent of a fine small European hotel. All rooms are furnished with antiques, and some have working fireplaces, four-poster beds, sauna, steam

bath and whirlpool baths. Outdoor swimming pool, too. A room in the Carriage House is a special treat. If you can't stay here, it's worth a visit just to see it.
66 Mount Desert St., Bar Harbor, ME 04609
(207) 288-4596, 1-800-274-5334
www.barharborvacations.com
email: barhbrinns@aol.com

• The Stratford House Inn — Bar Harbor
If Bar Harbor is your objective, but the Holiday Inn is not, try this elegant English Tudor Manor, built in 1900 by a wealthy publisher as his summer "cottage." Ten beautifully-decorated rooms, a dining room replete with original period furnishings, a library, veranda and even a music room (with a grand piano). Frenchman's Bay and Acadia National Park, of course, are within walking distance, as is the village itself, boasting 14 museums and more shops than you'll want to think about.
45 Mount Desert St., Bar Harbor, ME 04609
(207) 288-5189

• Captain Isaac Merrill Inn — Blue Hill
The original 1830 home of a seafaring captain, renovated (by his great-granddaughter) in 1994, this inn sits at the head of Blue Hill Bay. Offering the Captain's suite (boasting four-poster bed and kitchenette), assorted other rooms and a completely-equipped two-bedroom apartment.
Take Route 15 from Route 1 east of Bucksport.
One Union St., Blue Hill, ME 04614
(207) 374-2555, 1-800-374-2555
www.captainmerrillinn.com
email: imi@midmaine.com

• The Hideaway on Pocomoonshine Lake — South Princeton
A hunting and fishing dream come true. Three housekeeping cottages overlooking the lake, all completely equipped for extended visits (weekly minimum June through mid-September; two-night minimum during spring and fall). Use of boats and canoes included, but you have to net your own bass, perch, salmon and trout. Hunt during season in woods you have all to yourself (except for deer, et. al.). Three more large lakes nearby.
Take Route 179 north from Ellsworth to Aurora; take Route 9 to South Princeton.
29 The Hideaway Lane, So. Princeton, ME 04668
(207) 427-6183

Bed & Breakfasts

• Mira Monte Inn — Bar Harbor

Although situated in Bar Harbor, this special place is in a world of its own. Built in 1864, the house sits on two beautifully-landscaped acres, and features balconies and a great wrap-around porch. Luxury two-room suites have a parlor, fireplace, canopy beds, double-whirlpool baths, kitchenette and a private deck overlooking the gardens. Full breakfast buffet plus complimentary refreshments each afternoon.

169 Mt. Desert St., Bar Harbor, ME 04609
(207) 288-4263, 1-800-553-5109
www.miramonte.com
email: mburns@miramonte.com

• Anne's White Columns Inn — Bar Harbor

One way to escape downtown Bar Harbor is to duck into the columned portico of this elegant inn. A sparkling fire awaits you downstairs, and a comfy four-poster beckons you up. Package deals usually include discounts at area restaurants and attractions.

57 Mount Desert Street, Bar Harbor, ME 04609
(207) 288-5357, 1-800-321-6379
www.anneswhitecolumns.com
email: info@anneswhitecolumns.com

• Brewer House — Calais

An architectural treasure — a unique Greek Revival with columns front and back, French nine-over-nine windows, Grecian moldings, Ionic plaster, marble fireplaces, silver doorknobs and an elliptical staircase. A cozy three-room servants' quarters unit is also special. Proximity to Canada affords a "two-nation vacation," not to mention the highest tides in the continental U.S. Spectacular scenery and much to see and do, all far from the crowds.

Coastal Route 1, Calais/Robbinston, ME 04671
(207) 454-2385, 1-800-821-2028
www.mainerc.com/brewer.html

On the Islands

Inns & Lodges

• Goose Cove Lodge — Sunset

On a hillside overlooking Penobscot Bay, Goose Cove is an informal, yet sophisticated inn on 21 acres of coastal forest inhabited by birds, lush fauna and wildlife. 22 cottages, suites and rooms, some with fireplaces, wrap-around sundecks and kitchenettes. Complete dining facilities plus outdoor café, and lobster feast on the beach every Monday (during summer season). Barred Island Preserve and Crockett Cove Woods are nearby. Uncounted islands in all directions, including Deer Isle, North Haven and Vinalhaven, Isle au Haut and Swans Island.

Route 1 to Orland. Turn south onto Route 175 to Sargentville. Then take Route 15 to Deer Isle and onto Sunset.
PO Box 40, Sunset, ME 04683
1-800-728-1963
www.goosecovelodge.com

• Tidewater Motel — Vinalhaven

A small motel tucked away in Carver's Harbor, the Tidewater offers eight waterfront rooms with decks. Five of the rooms have kitchenettes. A visit to Vinalhaven is a visit to Maine's seafaring past, and the local Historical Society Museum will provide all the necessary details. Lanes Island Reserve and Armbrust Hill Wildlife Reservation are both nearby. Galleries, shops and restaurants abound.

Take the ferry from Rockland. The island is also accessible by air.
PO Box 546, Vinalhaven, ME 04863
(207) 863-4618
www.foxislands.net/~twmotel
email: tidewater@foxislands.net

• The Island Inn — Monhegan Island

Dating from 1807, the inn overlooks Monhegan Harbor. Full dining facilities. 15 rooms and suites with private baths; 19 with shared baths. Easy access to the island's footpaths through pine forests and along dramatic cliffs. The island is most famous for its unique art colony, but it also boasts 600 species of wildflowers.

Take the ferry from either Boothbay Harbor, New Harbor or Port Clyde (reservations required).
PO Box 128, Monhegan Island, ME 04852
(207) 596-0371

www.islandinnmonhegan.com
email: islandin@midcoast.com

• Eggemoggin Landing — Little Deer Isle
  Modest facilities in a fabulous setting that invite boaters as well as landlubbers. Full dining facilities. Powerboat, kayak and bike rentals, sailing tours, lobsterboat excursions. 300-foot pier on Eggemoggin Reach. All rooms have water views.
  Take Route 15 through Blue Hill and on to Little Deer Isle.
Route 15, Little Deer Isle, ME
(207) 348-6115
email: eggland@acadia.net

• Tuckanuck Lodge — Matinicus Island
  Nestled on the end of a dead-end road is this small rustic inn — more like a B&B, but with full dining facilities. With only seven rooms, some with ocean views, it provides a nice base for exploring this unique island 23 miles out to sea. A puffin colony occupies Matinicus Rock in June and July each year. The island boasts a mere 60 year-round residents, mostly lobstermen and their families, although the bird population is enormous. Moorings available for boaters.
  Ferry from Rockland or fly from Boston or Rockland. If going by boat, call (207) 366-3610 to secure a mooring.
PO Box 217, Matinicus Island, ME 04851
(207) 366-3830

Kennebec & Moose River Valleys

Inns & Lodges

• Attean Lake Lodge — Jackman
  Secluded, private and undeveloped, the lodge is the only establishment on this beautiful lake in the mountains (actually on an island — a launch will bring you from shore). 15 comfortable log cabins with full baths, fireplaces and all the comforts — except for the use of kerosene lamps. Swimming, lake and river fishing, sailing, boating, hiking, mountain-climbing (watch for moose). Nearby tennis, white-river rafting, golf, seaplane rides. Full dining facilities. Two hours from Quebec City.
  Take Route 201 from Waterville north to Jackman, then turn left on Attean Road. Transfer to cabin cruiser for 5-minute ride to the island.
Jackman, ME 04945
(207) 668-3792

Moosehead Lake & Katahdin

Inns & Lodges

• Lodge at Moosehead Lake — Greenville
    Paradise for the outdoorsman — on a hill overlooking the lake and the Great North Woods — yet all five rooms and three suites have full baths, whirlpool tubs, fireplaces, TV/VCR and unbelievable sunsets thrown in by Mother Nature. Highly rated. Hiking, canoeing, kayaking, mountain-biking — or take the family on a Moose Safari.
    Take Route 6 off I-95 in Howland, continue through Milo, Dover-Foxcroft, Guilford, Monson and on to Greenville.
Upon Lily Bay Rd, Box 1167, Greenville, ME 04441
(207) 695-4400

• Greenville Inn
    Dine like a millionaire in a millionaire's mansion atop a hill with spectacular views of Moosehead Lake. Classic wood paneling, fireplaces, huge windows. The new cottages are modern and more than comfortable, and all sport panoramic mountaintop views of spectacular Moosehead Lake. The dining room serves meals many consider the best in the region.
    Route 15 north to Greenville. Turn right on Norris Street, the second street on the right after the flasher.
Box 1194, Norris Street, Greenville, ME 04441
(207) 695-2206 or 1-888-695-6000
www.greenvilleinn.com
email: gvlinn@moosehead.net

• The Blair Hill Inn — Greenville
    This 1891 Victorian mansion, at the top of Blair Hill amid 15 spectacular acres, sports eight rooms, four with fireplaces and all with private baths. Views of Moosehead Lake and the surrounding mountains are truly awe-inspiring, and there's even a view from the whirlpool tub on the porch overlooking the lake, as well. The inn is noted for its fine dining, which includes gourmet dishes, wood-grilled seafood and special dessert surprises. Afternoon tea is included as well as a sumptuous breakfast.
Lily Bay Road, PO Box 1288, Greenville, ME 04441
1-888-918-8880
www.blairhill.com
email: info@blairhill.com

Museums

Courtesy of Stanley Museum, Kingfield

Maine's illustrious history is preserved and shared in a wide variety of different museums, which can be found throughout the state. Although some are located in high-traffic tourist spots, many are situated in more off-the-beaten-track sites. In the case of the former, we suggest planning your visit on off-days or, at the least, during off-hours. Art museums are listed separately in The Visual Arts section and most nautical/marine museums are listed in the Boats & Boating section.

Southern Coastal

• Seashore Trolley Museum — Kennebunkport
    The world's largest and oldest (1939) museum of mass-transit vehicles, including electric trolleys, tours of carbarns and narrated rides.
195 Log Cabin Road, PO Box A bin, Kennebunkport, ME 04046
(207) 967-2712
www.trolleymuseum.org
email: carshop@gwi.net

• Sabbathday Lake Shaker Museum — New Gloucester
    27 exhibits in six buildings through which you can explore over 200 years of Shaker heritage in Maine. Located in a village that claims to be the only active Shaker community in the world.
707 Shaker Road, New Gloucester, ME 04260
(207) 926-4597
www.shaker.lib.me.us
email: usshakers@aol.com

Greater Portland

• Children's Museum of Maine — Portland
    Exhibits and programs to encourage the curiosity and learning of children of all ages. Lots of hands-on displays and lots of things to hold the interest of the younger set — space shuttle, computer lab, lobsterboat, more.
142 Free Street, Portland, ME 04101
(207) 828-1234

• Portland Head Light Museum — Cape Elizabeth
(207) 799-2661

Western Mountains & Lakes

• Rangeley Lakes Logging Museum — Rangeley
    Exhibits of folk art — woodcarving, painting, knitting — and oral history preserving the heritage of the timber industry in the western mountains of Maine. Also the site of the annual Logging Festival held the last full weekend in July.
PO Box 154, Rangeley, ME 04970
(207) 864-3939

• Jones Museum of Glass — Sebago
   An outstanding collection of more than 6,000 pieces of antique glass and china.
(207) 787-3370

• Wilhelm Reich Museum — Rangeley
   175 acres of woods and fields surrounding the two major buildings where
the work (on the energy function that governs all living organisms) of the
physician/scientist is presented and interpreted.
Dodge Pond Road, PO Box 687, Rangeley, ME 04970
(207) 864-3443
www.sometel.com/~wreich
email: WReich@Rangeley.org

• Stanley Museum — Kingfield
   Permanent tribute to the brothers F.E. and F.O. Stanley, whose invention of
the Stanley Steamer tipped the infant auto industry on its ear. Chansonetta
Stanley Emmons, a sister, was equally celebrated for her extraordinary photographs
of turn-of-the-century American life. Steam cars built in 1905, 1910 and 1916,
musical instruments, photography and family archives housed in a 1903
schoolhouse.
School Street, PO Box 280, Kingfield, ME 04947
(207) 265-2729
email: stanleym@somtel.com

Midcoast

• Bowdoin College Library Special Collections — Brunswick
   The Abbott Memorial, Nathaniel Hawthorne and Henry Wadsworth
Longfellow collections, fine-press volumes, manuscripts relating to the early
history of Maine and Massachusetts, the Civil War and reconstruction, Arctic
exploration. Some materials dating from as early as 1478.
1 College Station, Brunswick, ME 04011
(207) 725-3288
www.bowdoin.edu
email: library@bowdoin.edu

• Peary-MacMillan Arctic Museum — Brunswick
   Exhibits or artifacts and equipment from the polar expeditions of two
famous Bowdoin alumni — Robert E. Peary and Donald B. MacMillan. Displays
of Arctic animals and Inuit art and artifacts.

Hubbard Hall, Bowdoin College, Brunswick, ME 04011
(207) 725-3289
www.bowdoin.edu/dept/arctic
email: nwagner@henry.bowdoin.edu

• Joshua Chamberlain Museum — Brunswick
   Home of famous Civil War hero and Bowdoin College president. Two other museum buildings offer local history and seafaring/medical history, as well.
226 Maine Street, Brunswick, ME 04011
(207) 729-6606
www.curtislibrary.com/pejepscot.htm
Email: dasmith@gwi.net

• Musical Wonder House Music Museum — Wiscasset
   A collection of 18th-, 19th- and 20-Century instruments, music boxes and other ephemera in the musical vein housed in an 1852 sea-captain's mansion. Guided tours available. Admission charges start at $8.
(207) 882-7163

• Owls Head Transportation Museum — Owls Head
   Large collection of antique planes (some 28 at last count), autos (more than 50), steam engines, motorcycles, bicycles and carriages maintained in operating condition and demonstrated via a series of special events, including "Antique Aeroplane Shows" and numerous rallies throughout the summer and fall.
Route 73, PO Box 277, Owls Head, ME 04854 (two miles south of Rockland)
(207) 594-4418
www.ohtm.org
email: ohtm@midcoast.com

• Shore Village Museum — Rockland
   Lighthouse lovers will here find one of the largest collections of lighthouse memorabilia anywhere. Open June 1 through Oct. 15.
(207) 594-0311

• Conway Homestead-Cramer Museum — Rockport
   Hosted by the Camden-Rockport Historical Society, the Homestead-Cramer is an 18th-century restored/furnished homestead with barn, blacksmith shop, maple sugar house, herb garden and museum.
PO Box 747, Rockport, ME 04856
(207) 236-2257
email: chmuseum@mint.net

Down East

• Swans Island Lobster and Marine Museum — Swans Island
    History of the commercial fishing industry in Maine.
4 Quarry Pond Road, Swans Island, ME 04685
(207) 526-4423

• Hudson Museum — Orono
    Exhibits and programs focusing on anthropology — Peoples of Maine, the
Arctic, Southwest, Northwest Coast, Prehispanic Mesoamerica, Oceana, Africa
and Panama. Housed at the University of Maine Center for the Arts.
5746 Maine Center for the Arts
Orono, ME 04469-5746
(207) 581-1901
www.ume.maine.edu/~hudsonm/
email: stephen@maine.maine.edu

Kennebec & Moose River Valleys

• Maine State Museum — Augusta
    Maine's natural, environmental and early history exhibited — "This Land
Called Maine," "12,000 Years in Maine," et al. Other exhibits include fishing, ice
harvesting, lumbering, quarrying and shipbuilding. Regarded as one of the best
state museums in the country.
83 State House Station, Augusta, ME 04333
(207) 287-2301
www.mainestatemuseum.org
email: maine.museum@state.me.us

• Children's Discovery Museum — Augusta
    What to do with the kids when you get a rainy day.
265 Water Street, Augusta, ME 04330
(207) 622-2209

• Nowetah's American Indian Museum — New Portland
    American Indian art and artifacts.
Route 27, Box 40, New Portland, ME 04961-3821
(207) 628-4981
Email: nowetah@sofcom.com

M o o s e h e a d   L a k e   &   K a t a h d i n

• Moosehead Marine Museum — Greenville
    Exhibits focus on logging, the lumberman and the Maine Guide. Point of departure for the SS Katahdin, the 225-seat tour boat (originally a towboat for moving logs across the lake), which offers cruises on Moosehead Lake, including around Mt. Kineo. This boat is also available for charter, weddings and parties.
P.O. Box 1151, Greenville, ME 04441
(207) 695-2716
www.katahdincruises.com

• The Lumberman's Museum — Patten
    Some 4,000 artifacts on display in nine buildings — tools of the trade plus a blacksmith shop, lumber camp, bateaux.
    Located on Shin Pond Road near the entrance to Baxter State Park.

F a r   N o r t h

• The Museum of Modern Fashion — Island Falls
    A collection of antique clothing — men's, women's and children's — from pre-Victorian, Victorian and Edwardian eras. 14 rooms of displays, dressmaker shoppe, hat boutique, bridal room and more.
Located in the center of Island Falls.
Call (207) 862-3797 for an appointment.

• Nylander Museum of Natural History — Caribou
    The original collections of Olof Nylander plus other collections donated to the museum. Minerals, marine fossils, mollusks, shells, mounted animal specimens.
657 Main Street, PO Box 1062, Caribou, ME 04736
(207) 493-4209
www.nylandermuseum.org
email: nylander@mfx.net

Nature Centers & Wildlife Refuges, Reserves & Sanctuaries

Borestone Mountain Wildlife Sanctuary, courtesy of Gilsland Farm: Black Cow Photo

Some of Maine's most interesting and beautiful sites have long been recognized by natives and visitors alike. Best of all, they have been set aside and protected — for us and from us — so that you can visit them without worry that they'll become housing tracts, malls or otherwise ruined.

There are no waterslides here, no outlet stores, no hotels or restaurants — only the good earth, tended by Mother Nature. And you are welcome.

Southern Coastal

• Laudholm Farm — Wells

The Wells National Research Reserve at Laudholm Farm preserves 1,600 acres of fields, forests, wetlands and beach. A saltwater farm offering ongoing research, education and visitor programs. Endangered and threatened species are protected in this conjunction of the Little, Merriland and Webhannet rivers and the Atlantic Ocean.

Off Route 1 in Wells.

(207) 646-1555

www.sirius.com/~fitch/wells/farm/farm2.html

• Rachel Carson National Wildlife Refuge — Wells
  Saltmarshes, forests, tidal creeks and wetlands — a vital combination nourishing plants, birds and sea creatures interdependently. A carefully planned trail will put you in touch with them all and with Mother Nature herself in an unparalleled environmental haven.
  On Route 9 off Route 1 in Wells, just south of Kennebunk and just north of Laudholm Farm.
  (207) 646-9226
  www.mainebirding.net/rachelcarson/

• Scarborough Marsh Nature Reserve — Scarborough
  3,000-acre wildlife habitat with muskrat, mink, otter and deer, but particularly birds — waterfowl, egrets, herons, ibises and many species of shorebirds. Open seven days a week. Guided and self-guided walks and canoe tours. Weekly programs. Early-morning birding.
  Take Pine Point Road off Route 1 for 0.8miles.
  (207) 883-5100
  www.mainebirding.net/mas/sc-marsh.shtml
  email: envcenters@maineaudubon.org

• East Point Sanctuary, Wood & State Islands — 30 acres — Biddeford Pool
  One of the best birding spots in southern Maine — open meadows, shrub vegetation and rocky coastal headlands. Trails bring you close to red-throated loons, sea ducks, alcids, terns and other birds, which share the area with harbor seals and other wildlife. Accessible only by boat.

• Mast Landing Sanctuary — 140 acres — Freeport
  Located at the head of tide of the Harraseeket River estuary. 3.5 miles of trails through open fields, forest and marshlands with a millstream, dam and cascading falls.

Greater Portland

• Gilsland Farm Environmental Center — Falmouth
  Headquarters of the Maine Audubon Society, Gilsland Farm is but one of 17 sanctuaries totaling over 3,000 acres owned and managed by the Society. The Farm is 65-acres of salt marshes alongside the Presumpscot River, ideal for nature study, hiking and quiet reflection. Organized programs, miles of trails, visitors' center with Children's Discovery Room, exhibits, natural history information, and preserved farm buildings.

Take the causeway north from the East Deering section of Portland on Route 1. (207) 781-2330
www.mainebirding.net/mas/

• Fore River Sanctuary — 85-acres — Portland
At the head of the Fore River, with a two-mile trail system among salt marshes, hemlock ravines, red oak and pine highlands. Habitat for warblers, shorebirds and hawks as well as mink, otter, deer and more.

Western Mountains & Lakes

• Hunter Cove Sanctuary — Rangeley
Part of a state game preserve, Hunter Cove is home to bear, moose, bobcat, deer and coyote. Three miles of trails through cedar swamp, spruce-fir forest, poplars and pines along the shoreline of Rangeley Lake.

Midcoast

• Hamilton Sanctuary — 74 acres — West Bath
On a peninsula in the New Meadows River, with striking views of rugged, unspoiled marshes, coves, mud flats and open water. 1.5 miles of trails put you close to osprey, blue heron and a variety of other birds and animals.

• Witch Island Sanctuary — 18 acres — South Bristol
Peripheral trail offers extraordinary views of Johns Bay.

• Josephine Newman Sanctuary — 119 acres — Georgetown
Bounded on two sides by salt marsh, the sanctuary has two miles of trails winding through stands of red oak, white pine, red spruce and hemlock, a beaver pond, cascading brook and rocky shore.

• Todd Wildlife Sanctuary — 364 acres, including Hog Island — Bremen

Down East

• Petit Manan National Wildlife Refuge — Milbridge
6,954-acre wildlife habitat, including 38 offshore islands spanning over 200 miles of coastline. Petit Manan, Franklin Island, Seal Island and Pond Island plus inland refuge areas in Steuben, Milbridge and Gouldsboro. Birdwatching, wildlife watching, hiking, some camping.

Take Route 1 northeast from Ellsworth
(207) 546-2124
www.llbean.com/parksearch/parks/html/15371gd.htm

• Fields Pond Nature Center — 192 acres — Holden

• Northeast Creek — 670 acres — Bar Harbor

• Moosehorn National Wildlife Refuge — 17,200 acres in Baring unit — Calais; 7,200 acres in Edmunds Unit — Cobscook Bay

The first in a chain of migratory bird refuges that extends from Maine to Florida. The Cobscook Bay has tidal fluctuations of 24 feet. In all, a highly glaciated expanse of large ledge outcrops, streams, lakes, bogs and marshes plus a diverse forest of aspen, maple, birch, spruce, white pine and fir. Wildlife includes the endangered American woodcock, bald eagle, black bear, deer, moose, ducks of many species, ospreys and river otter. 50 miles of trails. Some lakes open to fishing, but motor boats are prohibited.

Take Route 1 and just keep on going.
(207) 454-7161
www.mainebirding.net/mooshorn/

Moosehead Lake & Katahdin

• Borestone Mountain Wildlife Sanctuary — 1,634 acres — Elliotsville Township

Retreats & Spas for Body, Mind & Spirit

Courtesy of Living Water Spiritual Center, Winslow

Just coming to Maine is often a retreat from ordinary life. Simply being here can help your mind, body and spirit. You can enhance this natural healing process at our special retreats, spas and therapy centers. By catering to your physical, emotional and spiritual needs you can more fully relax and enjoy yourself. Go ahead — deepen your Maine experience.

Greater Portland

• Polarity Realization Institute — Portland

Home of RYSE (Realizing Your Sublime Energies), designed to allow people to take conscious control of their own energy systems to lead more aligned, fulfilled and productive lives. Offers education on understanding your energetic systems and how to use them to affect your emotional state and find personal power. Student clinic offers 1-1/2 hour sessions in Holistic Massage, Therapeutic Massage and Polarity Realization Therapy.

222 St. John Street, Suite 301, Portland, ME 04101

(207) 773-3028 or 1-800-262-8530

www.holistic-massage.com

email: Admissions@ryse.com

• River Yoga and Movement Center — Westbrook

Dance and Hatha yoga including Iyengar and Kripalu yoga are featured in this 2000-square-foot center overlooking the Saccarappa Falls of the Presumpscot River. Dana Warp Mill Complex, 90 Bridge Street, Suite 420, Westbrook, ME 04092 (207) 856-7962
www.riveryoga.com

• Akari Hair Care and Day Spa — Portland

Hair styling, color, facials, glycolic skin treatment, waxing, massage, reflexology, seaweed wrap, Moor mud mask, body herbal hot pack treatments and more are available in half- and full-day sessions.
Akari Hair Care and Day Spa
468-470 Fore Street, Portland, ME 04101
(207) 772-9060 or 1-877-890-0772
www.akarihairspa.com
email: info@akarihairspa.com

• The Yoga Center — Portland

The Center offers yoga instruction based primarily on the Iyengar technique, the type often recommended as a tool in relieving back pain, neck or shoulder tension and other physical problems. Center teachers also have experience with other forms of yoga including Astanga, Kripalu and classical Hatha. Instruction is offered in two studios.
137 Preble Street (near Portland Public Market), Portland, ME 04101
(207) 774-9642
www.maineyoga.com

Western Mountains & Lakes

• Nurture Through Nature — Naples

Holistic outdoor retreats and excursions for women only combining hiking, skiing or snowshoeing, backpacking, kayaking, canoeing and camping with workshops, meditations, yoga, inner-world explorations and group- and team-cohesiveness sessions. Various locations — Mooselookmeguntic Lake, West Branch of the Penobscot, Hiram, Bridgton — offer true back-to-nature settings. Retreats are designed to assure comfort and safety regardless of participants' fitness, age or experience.
RR #2, Box 550F, Naples, ME 04055
(207) 787-2379
email: ntn@pivot.net

• Maine Healing Arts Festival — Freedom
The Annual Maine Healing Arts Festival is a four-day, three-night Spiritual Community gathering featuring workshops, ceremonies and events. Each day begins with early-morning meditation with workshops on transformation and healing. Special events include a firewalk and sweat lodge. Opportunities for intensive and mini-workshops. Located at Hidden Valley Camp, Freedom, ME.
PO Box 288, Buckfield, ME 04220
(207) 336-2065 or (617) 492-3821
www.mainehealingarts.com
email: registration@mainehealingarts.com

• Northern Pines — Raymond
Relaxation and serenity served up among tall pines, clean air and the clear waters of Crescent Lake near Raymond. Essentially a B&B, but with vegetarian breakfasts plus massage therapy, salt glow aromatherapy, Moor body wraps, foot reflexology, transformational breath sessions, herbal facials and more. Or just relax and enjoy swimming or canoeing on the lake or hiking in the surrounding mountains.
P.O. Box 210, Brownfield, ME 04010 (winter)
31 Big Pine Road, Raymond, ME 04071 (summer)
(207) 935-7579 (winter), or (207) 655-7624 (summer)
www.maine.com/norpines/
email: norpines@pivot.net

• Mahoosuc Mountain Massage — Bethel
Therapeutic massage with two therapists with a medical and athletics background offer Swedish, NMT, on-site, Sports massage.
Box 933, Route 26, Bethel, ME 04217
(207) 824-4521

Midcoast

• Body Prayers — Camden
Restorative yoga retreats for women that blend Hatha yoga, meditation, quietude and "empty time" to restore natural inner rhythms. Enjoy vegetarian meals prepared by cooks schooled in the art of fine vegetarian cuisine. Also, weekend seminars and a couples' yoga retreat.
PO Box 448, Camden, ME 04843
1-888-666-6412
www.bodyprayers.com
email: patricia@bodyprayers.com

• Lakeshore Inn — Rockland

Pampered weekends for ladies are the featured offering. Amenities include a hands-on reflexology class, a professional speaker on Dreams, Energy and Stress, fluffy robes and relaxing in front of a fire or soaking in the enclosed, outdoor hot tub. The weekend also includes Body/Mind exercise, facials, manicure, paraffin wax treatment, massage, pedicure and a chef-prepared candlelight dinner.

184 Lakeview Drive (ME Route 17), Rockland, ME 04841

(207) 594-4209

email: lakshore@midcoast.com

Kennebec & Moose River Valleys

• Living Water Spiritual Center — Winslow

A variety of group and individual retreats designed to provide solitude for listening to the "Voice of God in your heart." Directed, silent retreats with an assigned spiritual director, solitude retreats with no planned activities, thematic retreats for groups and private retreats for individuals seeking solitude for reflection and prayer — on a beautiful, tranquil campus.

93 Halifax Street, Winslow, ME 04901

(207) 872-2370

www.e-livingwater.org

email: info@e-livingwater.org

The Performing Arts

Courtesy of Bangor Symphony Orchestra

It's true that Maine has a small population spread out over a vast area. But if you think that causes Mainers to neglect the performing arts, you would be wrong. More than a dozen performing arts theaters dot the Maine landscape, and offer a variety of more than 60 dramas and musicals each season. If you enjoy stage productions, but don't relish standing elbow-to-elbow with theatergoers in Boston or New York, the Pine Tree State troupers bring it all to you right here in Maine.

Maine also has two superb symphony orchestras, numerous chamber music groups, an opera repertory company, a world class orchestral school, a world-renown Gilbert and Sullivan company and a ballet company. Just to keep things interesting, we also have a performing steel band that is believed to be the largest north of the Caribbean!

Enjoy our celebration of life through Maine's Performing Arts.

Southern Coastal

Theater

• Ogunquit Playhouse — Ogunquit
    This is a beautiful summer stock theater — on the "straw-hat" circuit — with

dramatic and musical productions with world-class performers. Productions like Dracula, 42nd Street, Joseph and the Amazing Technicolor Dreamcoat and I Love You, You're Perfect, Now Change. Check for current offerings
PO Box 915, Ogunquit, ME 03907
(207) 646-5511
email: mail@ogunquitplayhouse.org

• Hackmatack Playhouse — Berwick
    A "set in the woods" playhouse experience. Summer stock productions of such classics as Damn Yankees, Godspell, The King and I, Sylvia and Wait Until Dark. Summer Drama Camps and Children's Theater productions, too. Check for current offerings.
Rts. 538 & 9W, Berwick, ME
(207) 698-1807
www.hackmatack.org/home.htm
email: hackplayhouse@aol.com

• Maine Stage Company — Springvale
    Quality, affordable entertainment in the southern Maine hills, coupled with great community involvement. This company produces many benefits for The Heart Foundation, Caring Unlimited — A Shelter for Battered Women, Make-A-Wish and other fine causes. It also helps underwrite theater arts education for interested and worthy young people. Productions like What the Rabbi Saw, Annie, The Odd Couple, and Prelude to a Kiss. Season runs from May to December. Check for current offerings.
PO Box 486, Springvale, ME 04086
(207) 324-9691
www.sanfordmainestage.com

Greater Portland

Theater

• Lyric Music Theater — South Portland
    This energetic community theater produces quality musicals like Gypsy, A Chorus Line, Wizard of Oz and High Society. The season runs from September to May. Check for current offerings.
176 Sawyer Street, South Portland, ME 04106
(207) 799-1421
www.lyricmusictheater.com
email: mrkeys@maine.rr.com

• Mad Horse Theater — Portland

The Mad Horse company was formed in 1986 under the guidance of Artistic Director Michael Rafkin. It consists of a small group of resident artists who share a vision — the production of high quality, intimate and provocative theatre as an ensemble. Intense portrayals of the human condition are reflected in productions such as One Flew Over the Cuckoo's Nest, Goodnight Desdemona, Who's Afraid of Virginia Wolf? and Angels in America.

92 Oak Street, Box 9715-343, Portland, ME 04104

www.madhorse.com

email: ansf@javanet.com

• Portland Stage Company

This is classic theater with outstanding professional productions. Everything from Moliere's The Misanthrope to Harold Pinter's Betrayal and on to A Perfect Ganesh, ART, Gaslight, Wit, Leaving Queens and A Christmas Carol. Check for current listings.

PO Box 1458, 25A Forest Avenue (in the Arts District), Portland, ME 04101

Tel: (207) 774-0465

Fax: (207) 774-0576

www.portlandstage.com

portstage@aol.com

Music

Courtesy of Portland Symphony Orchestra

• Portland Symphony Orchestra

Maine is blessed with several fine orchestras, foremost of which is the world-class Portland Symphony Orchestra, directed by Toshiyuki Shimada. The PSO offers a full schedule of concerts in Merrill Auditorium in Portland from

October through April each year, many featuring guest artists from the leading orchestras of the world as well as Broadway stars.

The Merrill has been beautifully restored; the acoustics are excellent, yet it is small enough for the audience to feel real intimacy with this superb orchestra. The Portland Symphony Orchestra offers top-quality music without having to be heard through amplification or seen through opera glasses.

The PSO also traditionally offers a series of Independence Pops concerts, which are scheduled around the state during the week preceding the Fourth of July. Venues are usually in Fort Williams Park in Cape Elizabeth; at Central Maine Technical College in Auburn; at Shawnee Peak in Bridgton; at Thornton Academy in Saco; and at Southern Maine Technical College in South Portland.

Another highlight each season is the annual Christmas Concert, which is offered at several performances at the Merrill in mid-December.

Contact the PSO for specific times, dates and to confirm locations.
Portland Symphony Orchestra, PO Box 3573, 477 Congress Street, Portland, ME 04104-3573
Ticket sales: PortTix, 20 Myrtle Street, Portland, ME 04101
(207) 842-0800
On-line ticket sales: www.portlandsymphony.com

• Portland Opera Repertory Theatre (PORT)

The Portland Opera Theatre performances are also in the beautiful Merrill Auditorium. A special "road" production tours other venues throughout greater Portland, including Peak's Island. Performances are typically during the months of July and August. Past works have included Mozart's Marriage of Figaro and Rossini's Barber of Seville with Faust a likely next staging. Check for current offerings, dates, times and locations.
PORT, PO Box 7733, 477 Congress Street, Portland, ME 04112
Tel: (207) 879-7678
Fax: (207) 879-7681
www.portopera.org
email: portopera@aol.com

• Chamber Music Festival — Portland

Another musical treat is the Portland Chamber Music Festival, which offers a series of concerts in August. These performances are enhanced by many visiting musicians of national and international prominence, and are frequently featured on both Maine Public Radio and National Public Radio. Information on specific dates and venues are available from festival officials.

Portland Chamber Music Festival, Westbrook College Campus, University of New England, Stevens Avenue, Portland, ME 04103
(800) 320-0257
www.pcmf.org
Email: Jennifer.elowitch@verizon.net

Dance

• The Portland Ballet Company (PBC)
　　The Portland Ballet is a small, classically-based company founded in 1985. Under the direction of Eugenia L. O'Brien, PBC has presented both classics and contemporary works including The Silver Seal, Arthur Rex, Carmina Burena, Dreambirds, Summer Wind, Peter and the Wolf, Bolero and Swan Lake. PBC has a repertoire of over 25 ballets offered in various indoor and outdoor venues. Check for current offerings, dates, times and locations.
The Portland Ballet, 517 Forest Avenue, Suite 2, Portland, ME 04101
Tel: (207) 772-9671
www.portlandballet.org
email: info@portlandballet.org

Western Mountains & Lakes

Theater

• The Public Theatre — Lewiston-Auburn
　　Contemporary dramatic and comedic productions (i.e., Neil Simon's Rumors) in the historic Ritz Theater.
Two Great Falls Plaza, Auburn, ME 04210
(207) 782-3200
email: thepublictheatre@aol.com

• The Celebration Barn — South Paris
　　A barn on 10 acres set in the foothills of western Maine houses one of the state's most unusual schools. Since 1972, Tony Montanaro and The Celebration Barn have provided workshops for mime, dance, improvisation, and storytelling. The Barn offers visiting performers, productions and instruction. Learn comedy, juggling, slapstick, more. There are public performances throughout the summer so check for offerings.
190 Stock Farm Road
Tel: (207) 743-8452

Fax: (207) 743-3889
www.celebrationbarn.com
email: info@celebrationbarn.com

Midcoast

Theater

• The Chocolate Church Youth Theater — Bath
There is much to entertain you year round in this former wooden church painted chocolate (what else?) Classes, workshops, children's theater and productions of such fare as Annie, The Wizard of Oz, Peter Pan, Camelot, and Saffire — The Uppity Blues Woman. Performing artists scheduled throughout the winter. Check for current offerings.
Tel: (207) 443-8455
Fax: (207) 442-8455
www.chocolatechurcharts.org
email: chocolatechurch@suscom-maine.net

• Maine State Music Theater — Brunswick
Professional musical theater with productions like The King & I, Chicago, Ragtime and She Loves Me. Season runs June through August. Check for current offerings.
14 Maine Street, Suite 109, Brunswick, ME 04011
Tel: (207) 725-8769
Fax: (207) 725-1199
www.msmt.org
email: info@msnt.org

Music

• Bay Chamber Concerts — Rockport and Camden
The Bay Chamber Concert series annually features a wide variety of different music styles — from jazz to chamber music, folk music, music with an international flavor, choral presentations and more. Two venues — the Rockport Opera House and the Strom Auditorium in Camden. Pre-concert talks by the musicians, special activities for young music lovers and both afternoon and evening concerts throughout the year.
Bay Chamber Concerts. P.O. Box 228, Rockport, ME 04856
(207) 236-2823
www.baychamberconcerts.org

Down East

Theater

• Penobscot Theatre Company — Bangor
    Shakespeare in Maine? You bet! This is home to the Maine Shakespeare Festival. Fire-torch jugglers, Renaissance singers and dancers, sword duels accompany productions such as The Little Prince, King Lear, Servant of Two Masters and Twelfth Night presented under starlit skies. Winter season productions also. Check for current listings.
163 Main Street, Bangor, ME 04401
Tel: (207) 942-3333 (Box Office)
Tel: (207) 947-6618 (Adm. Office)
Fax: (207) 947-6678
http://ptc.maineguide.com
email: ptcmsf@mint.net

• Acadia Repertory Theatre — Somesville
    Summer season entertainment for the whole family. Children's offerings like The Hobbit and adult fare such as Murder at the Howard Johnson's, The Picture of Dorian Gray, The Foreigner and The Unexpected Guest. Check for current listings.
PO Box 106, Mt. Desert, ME 04660
Located at the Masonic Hall, Rt. 102, Somesville
Tel: (207) 244-7260
email: arep@acadia.net

• Criterion Theatre — Bar Harbor
    You will have to contend with the traffic of Bar Harbor to attend a production here, but the architecture itself may be worth it. This is an 892-seat theatre built in 1932 in original Art Deco Style, recently renovated top to bottom. You might want to sit in the spectacular "floating balcony" with its nine separate, half-walled and curtained loges. The Criterion was on the vaudeville circuit for many years and was also designed to feature motion pictures. Today the Criterion offers films, live artist performances and theater productions throughout the year. Check for current offerings.
35 Cottage Street, Bar Harbor, ME 04609
Tel: (207) 288-3441 or (207) 288-5829
www.criteriontheatre.com
info@criteriontheatre.com

• The Grand Auditorium — Ellsworth

Ellsworth is a town full of pleasant surprises and The Grand Auditorium is no exception. This comfortable 550-seat theater is home to movies, live artistic performances and dramatic and musical productions. It's also the current home of The Gilbert and Sullivan Society of Hancock County. That's noteworthy because when this company competed in a worldwide G&S competition in Buxton, England, in 1994, they took first place. Can you imagine that — Americans — from Maine no less — taking first place — in England! Recent productions have included 1776, Lost in Yonkers, A Chorus Line and from the G&S Company — Pirates of Penzance and Ruddigore. Check for current offerings.
PO Box 941, Main Street, Ellsworth, ME 04605
Tel: (207) 667-5911
Fax: (207) 667-6605
http://w2.downeast.net/thegrand/
email: thegrand@downeast.net
for G&S info: Dave Blanchette, The G&S Society of Hancock County, PO Box V, Ellsworth, ME 04605

Music

• Bangor Symphony Orchestra

The BSO is the oldest community orchestra in continuous operation in the United States, and it's still going strong after well over 100 years. Offerings include classical concerts, family casual concerts, pops concerts, special holiday events (Nutcracker "event," with the Robinson Ballet, at the Maine Discovery Museum) and outreach concerts in various venues around the state.

Following the departure of conductor Christopher Zimmerman, after seven very successful seasons, the orchestra will be hosting a number of guest conductors through next season, all of whom bring impressive credentials and heightened enthusiasm to the orchestra. Check for current offerings.
Bangor Symphony Orchestra, 44 Central Street, P.O. Box 1441, Bangor, ME 04402
(207) 942-5555 or (800) 639-3221
www.bangorsymphony.com
symphony@bangorsymphony.com

• The Pierre Monteux School — Hancock

The Pierre Monteux School for Conductors and Orchestra Musicians, established by the renown conductor and violist, holds a series of concerts during the summer featuring world-class musicians and conductors. Programs include symphony concerts, chamber music, children's concerts and pops concerts. This school, now in its sixth decade of existence, is a true jewel, the distinguished alumni of which include Erich Kunzel, Lorin Mazel, Sir Neville Marriner and Andre Previn. Its tradition of excellence is being carried on by Music Director Michael Jinbo, who has performed (on violin) with musical groups as diverse as the St. Petersburg Ballet in Russia and the Cab Calloway orchestra. Enjoy an evening of exquisite music in a simple sylvan setting.

The Pierre Monteux School, P.O. Box 157, Hancock, ME 04640-0157

(207) 422-3931

Email: pmonteux@aol.com

• Flash In The Pan — Blue Hill Peninsula

If you find yourself on the Blue Hill Peninsula on a Monday night between Memorial Day and Labor Day, don't miss this steel band. This eclectic group of steel drummers numbering 35-40 may be the largest such band north of the Caribbean. Under Music Director Carl Chase they create a magical sound that is a magnet for community fun. Enjoy the spontaneous dancing, or better still, get up and dance yourself. Venues change throughout the season. Carl is also director for several youth groups and you may have an opportunity to hear them too. Check for current offerings.

Flash In The Pan

www.peninsulapan.org

cchase@acadia.net

Kennebec & Moose River Valleys

Theater

• The Theater at Monmouth

The Theater at Monmouth combines wonderful architecture with outstanding performances. Productions are held at Cumston Hall, an architectural gem listed on the National Register of Historic Sites in 1976. This is a Maine heavyweight in Shakespearean theater — and other classics like Private Lives, The Matchmaker, H.M.S. Pinafore, Cymbeline, plus Midsummer Madness. Spring children's classics also. Check for current listings.

PO Box 385, Monmouth, ME 04259-0385

Tel: (207) 933-2952 (Box Office)

Tel: (207) 933-2952 (Bus. Office)

www.theateratmonmouth.com

email: TAMOffice@TheaterAtMonmouth.org

• Lakewood Theater — Skowhegan

Lakewood Theater bills itself as "Maine's Summer Theater," and, since it has been refining its craft for over 100 years, that sounds very reasonable. From May to September you can expect a wide offering of shows such as Oliver, The Secret Garden, The Roaring 20s Shrew, Lafferty's Wake and Running in the Red. Lakewood also offers Young Performers Camp Productions like The Three Little Pigs and Zink: The Myth, The Legend, The Zebra. Check for current offerings.

6 miles north of Skowhegan on Rt. 201

Tel: (207) 474-7176

www.lakewoodtheater.org

email: lakewoodtheatrer@hotmail.com

The Visual Arts

"Fish Houses and Beach" by Samuel Peter Rolt Triscott.
Courtesy of Farnsworth Art Museum, Rockland

There is no end to the beauty of Maine, a fact recognized for many years by those who see with exceptional vision. Many of the artists who painted in Maine in the nineteen and twentieth centuries came to Maine as visitors to art colonies such as Monhegan Island or Ogunquit. Others simply came as summer visitors in various communities throughout the state. Some returned year after year, and some made Maine their permanent home. There seems to be no end to the artists who have chosen to paint in the tranquility and unique and inspiring light that bathes Maine. Among them are Winslow Homer, Fitz Hugh Lane, Charles Woodbury, Henry Strater, Thomas Cole, Fredrick Edwin Church, Marguerite Zorach, Childe Hassam, Pegy Bacon, Louise Nevelson, Walt Kuhn and generations of Wyeths.

Maine's love affair with art is hardly limited to Maine-inspired art, however, and extensive collections from all over the globe can be found in major art museums and centers spread throughout the state. You can indulge yourself here in a moveable feast of Cezanne, Gilbert Stuart, Degas, Mary Cassatt, Picasso, John Singleton Copley, Renoir and the ancient art of Assyria, Greece, Rome and Asia.

Outdoor sculpture, too, seems much at home in Maine and the landscape is dotted with outstanding pieces in classic and contemporary form. Obviously we can't list all of them, but we do point out a few pieces we think will interest you. Keep your eye out as you travel, because in Maine, they're often where you would least expect them.

Of course film is a large part of the visual arts and it seems that in recent years Maine has caught the film flu from our good neighbors in southern New Hampshire. Very rapidly we are becoming a film Mecca with an annual international festival in Waterville and another one underway in Portland.

The Visual Arts await you in Maine. All you need do is look.

Southern Coastal

Art Museums & Centers

• Ogunquit Museum of American Art

This museum has been called "the most beautiful small museum in the world," and rightly so. Art, architecture, setting and a spectacular ocean view create an exceptional confluence of beauty. The Museum is dedicated exclusively to 20th century American art and houses over 1,300 of the nation's most important paintings, sculpture, drawings and prints. Among the distinguished artists who have worked in Ogunquit (which means "Beautiful place by the sea") are Marsden Hartley, Edward Hopper and Walt Kuhn.

The season runs from July 1 to September 30 and the museum is open Mon.-Sat., 10:30am to 5pm. In nearby Perkins Cove you will find many small galleries that continue the artistic heritage of Ogunquit.
183 Shore Road, Ogunquit, ME 03907
(207) 646-4909

Outdoor Sculpture

• Sacrifices of War, 1925 — Kittery
Leave Portsmouth, New Hampshire, via the Rt. 1 Memorial Bridge and you will immediately see this monument. This bronze by Russian-born Bashka Paeff (1893-1979) illustrates the sacrifices made by soldiers and sailors. It depicts a woman shielding a child from the raging surf of war while below her, two men and a dog have succumbed to the waters. Behind the woman, files of soldiers march in and out of the waters. Paeff's career spanned the major tragedies of this century, but this Kittery monument was one of her first large commissions. Governor Percival Baxter praised Paeff for the monument's focus on life, but shortly before its dedication, Paeff had to tone down pacifist implications of the suffering of the men marching into and out of the waters.

Greater Portland

Art Museums & Centers

• Portland Museum of Art — Portland
The first thing that strikes you about the Portland Museum of Art is the 1983 Charles Shipman Payson building designed by Henry Nichols Cobb of I.M. Pei & Partners. He designed it with the intention that "...masterpieces of the State of Maine collection, beyond being simply made available to the public, should be appropriately celebrated by the setting in which they are displayed." He succeeded.
The museum houses a diverse collection of fine and decorative arts from the 18th century to the present. A year-round array of special exhibitions and programs offers a view of American and European masterpieces including works by Mary Cassatt, Frederic Church, Edgar Degas, Marsden Hartley, Winslow Homer, Childe Hassam, Claude Monet, Pablo Picasso, Pierre-Auguste Renoir, Neil Welliver and William and Marguerite Zorach.
Also showcased in its landmark five-story building is Maine's exceptional contribution to American Art. Of special note is a body of 19 significant works by Winslow Homer.
The Museum is open Tues., Wed., Sat., Sun., 10am to 5pm and Thurs., Fri., 10am to 9pm.
Seven Congress Square, Portland, ME 04101
(207) 775-6148
www.portlandmuseum.org

Outdoor Sculpture

• Longfellow Monument (1888) — Portland
   Sculptor Franklin Simmons (1839-1913) was perhaps best known for the pieces he sculpted for the Senate Vice Presidential Bust Collection. Hannibal Hamlin of Maine and former Vice President of the United States was asked to select a sculptor to depict him, and he, in turn, designated Maine artist Simmons. Simmons was subsequently commissioned for busts of Vice Presidents Adlai Ewing Stevenson and Charles Warren and other dignitaries.
   Gaze on this colossal bronze set on a granite base at the corner of State and Congress Street and perhaps you will understand how Simmons viewed the towering mind that wrote of Paul Revere, Hiawatha and Evangeline.

• Our Lady of Victories (1891) — Portland
   In 1883 the Portland Soldiers & Sailors Monument Association was formed to raise funds to commemorate the Civil War. Local sculptor Franklin Simmons was again commissioned to cast the massive bronze. The statue depicts a stately, garlanded Lady of Victories standing serenely, yet with a vigilant gaze to the horizon. Richard Hunt, a prominent New York architect designed the massive stone pedestal. On the left side of the pedestal is a bronze casting of soldiers and, on the right side, a bronze casting of sailors, both in Civil War era uniforms.

Film

• Portland Festival of World Cinema
   Festival scheduled for October. Call for current offerings, dates, times and venues
39 Exchange Street, Suite 301, Portland, ME 04101
Tel: (207) 772-9234
Fax: (207) 772-9239
www.filmmaine.com
email: PFWC@moviemaker.com

Western Mountains & Lakes

Art Museums & Centers

• Bates College Museum of Art — Lewiston
   Historic Bates College houses one of the region's most impressive collections of masterworks on paper gracing the halls of its Museum of Art. Prints, drawings,

photographs and painting are all part of the collection. The centerpiece of the collection is a body of work and memorabilia created by Lewiston's most famous artist, Marsden Hartley.

The Museum also showcases exhibitions of contemporary art in its upper gallery, and serves as a major learning resource to Bates College and the surrounding area.

The Museum is open Tues. - Sat., 10am to 5pm, Sun., 1pm to 5pm and admission is free.

75 Russell Street, Bates College, Lewiston, ME 04240

(207) 786-6158

www.bates.edu/acad/museum

Midcoast

Art Museums & Centers

• Bowdoin College Museum of Art — Brunswick

At Bowdoin College, the Museum preserves some of the world's oldest artistic treasures including those of ancient Assyria, Greece, Rome and Asia. The collection also includes European and American paintings, sculpture, drawings, prints and photographs, representing a broad range of nations and time periods.

A temporary exhibition program frequently houses contemporary art, designed to place the permanent collection in a larger context.

The Museum is open Tues. - Sat., 10am to 5pm, Sun., 2pm to 5pm and admission is free.

Walker Art Building, Bowdoin College, Brunswick, ME, 04011

(207) 725-3275

www.bowdoin.edu/cwis/resources/museums.html

• Center for Maine Contemporary Art — Rockport

Here's where you go to see works by some of the best Maine artists — often emerging artists not seen elsewhere. The works are housed in a historic building with three floors of gallery space. CMCA is committed to advancing contemporary art in Maine and you will likely be impressed.

The gallery is open Tues. - Sat., 10am to 5pm, Sun. 12pm to 5pm.

162 Russell Avenue, Rockport, ME 04856

www.artsmaine.org

• Farnsworth Art Museum — Rockland

The Farnsworth is recognized as one of the finest regional art museums in the country and should not be missed. The Farnsworth focuses on the incredible art of Maine, whether created in, or simply inspired by, Maine. On exhibit are works by Fitz Hugh Lane, George Bellows, Winslow Homer, Rockwell Kent, John Marin and Louise Nevelson.

The Museum also houses a separate Wyeth Center, devoted to the art of the "first family" of Maine painting. This is where to see the many works of N.C., Andrew and Jamie Wyeth.

The Museum is open from Memorial Day to Columbus Day, daily 9am to 5pm and from Columbus Day to Memorial Day, Tues. - Sat., 10am to 5pm, Sun. 1:00p - 5:00p.
356 Main Street, Rockland, ME 04841
(207) 596-6457
wwwlfarnsworthmuseum.org

Outdoor Sculpture

• The Lobsterman, 1939 — Bailey Island
Go down Rt. 24 to the tip at Land's End Gift Shop to see this realistic sculpture. Local lobsterman Elroy Johnson posed for this sculpture, which depicts the claw pegging (immobilizing) of a lobster. Lebanese-born artist Victor Kahill created the plaster model for the 1939 World's Fair, but funds for a metal casting were lacking. When Johnson died in 1973, the community raised the funds for three castings. One is in downtown Portland, another at the National Park Service headquarters in Washington, D.C. This one is especially dedicated to all fishermen and is situated only feet from the waters that Johnson worked.

• Pioneer Family, 1964 — Waldoboro
This is a stylized bronze sculpture with a great story. It depicts a father and older daughter gazing to the horizon while mother and young son are engaged in reading a book.

William Zorach (1889-1966) was a well-established sculptor when he created the model of the piece for the 1936 Texas Centennial Competition. He received first prize and was about to create a full-scale sculpture when some astute Texans noticed that all the figures were naked and further, that the mother was not wearing a wedding ring. This not only cost Zorach the prize, but the sculpture was not cast for almost 30 years.

This is one of two existing casts of Pioneer Family. This one came to Maine when Sam and Sally Pennington, owners and publishers of Maine Antiques Digest, purchased it at a Christie's auction. It is the centerpiece of a small sculpture garden outside the Digest offices. The figures remain unclothed and the woman still does not have a wedding band, but the people here in Maine don't seem to mind.

• Andre the Seal, 1978 — Rockport
    Just turn down into Marine Park at Rockport Harbor and drive to the water's edge to see Andre. This is a sculpture for all the family — one that commemorates a wonderful story. Rockport lobsterman Harry Goodridge found Andre abandoned in Penobscot Bay. He raised the seal, taught him tricks and sent him to Boston's New England Aquarium each winter. In spring, Andre would return, swimming the 150 miles to Rockport. He jumped aboard boats for food, did tricks for the tourists, followed divers underwater and won the heart of the town. He and Goodridge were even named townspeople of the year. Lincolnville sculptor Jane Wasey (1912-1992) sculpted this granite version of Andre in 1978. Andre was there to help pull the chord, unveiling his very own likeness.

Down East

Art Museums & Centers

• University of Maine Museum of Art — Orono
    Thanks largely to grants from Andrew Carnegie, the University of Maine has the state's only citizen-owned museum with a permanent fine arts collection. The Museum was established with the goal of educating the public about art's histories and cultural meanings. The Museum ensures that the 5,700-piece collection is available to the public by routinely rotating 20 percent to display in public spaces.
    Highlights of the collection include works by Winslow Homer, Max Beckmann, Francisco Goya, George Inness, Kathe Kollwitz and Pablo Picasso. The Museum also offers a significant body of contemporary art, featuring works on paper by Jim Dine, David Hockney, Roy Lichtenstein and Elizabeth Murray.
    Summer hours are Mon. - Sat., 9am to 4pm and admission is free.
University of Maine Museum of Art, 5712 Carnegie Hall, Orono, ME 04469

Outdoor Sculpture

• I Am The Way, 1998 — Blue Hill
    This abstract granite structure is at the corner of Union and High Streets at George Stevens Academy and is a real traffic stopper. This cairn-like composition of stones is a 10-foot high representation of a human figure. Its outstretched arms point neither to the school nor the street — suggesting to the students that they must find their own way. Stevens Academy commissioned the sculpture in honor

of its 100th anniversary. Castine artist Clark Fitz-Gerald made sure the figure was a local by using granite from an old quarry in East Blue Hill. Perhaps this figure can provide some direction to all that view it.

• Stonecutter, c. 1950 — Stonington
At the public landing in Stonington you will find this life-like bronze figure of a stonecutter. William Muir (1902-1964) is best known for abstract organic wood sculpture. However, he lived the last 50 years of his life here and was deeply connected to the workers who cut the stone from the nearby quarries. The depicted bronze stonecutter is set on the granite he is cutting; and he clearly knows his craft. Shorn of shirt, with a rakishly-set cap, he hammers in a relaxed yet highly focused manner. He knows both the product he is likely to produce and the danger to stone and self should his attention slip. On the 30th anniversary of Muir's death, a former stone worker donated this sculpture as a memorial.

Kennebec & Moose River Valleys

Art Museums & Centers

• Colby Museum of Art — Waterville
The Colby Museum of Art offers an outstanding view of American art from the early 18th century through to the present. The collection includes important early portraiture by John Singleton Copley, Gilbert Stuart and Charles Willson Peale. In addition, the Jette' Collection also features 96 works by American Impressionists.

The Museum also showcases the work of significant 20th century American artists, many of whom lived or worked in Maine. These include John Marin, Fairfield Porter, George Bellows and Alex Katz. The 13 galleries of the new Lunder Wing will exhibit works that trace the development of American art from the mid-18th century into the early 20th century.

The Museum if open Mon. - Sat., 10am to 12pm; 1pm to 4:30pm, Sun., 2pm to 4:30pm and admission is free.
Colby College, Waterville, ME 04901
(207) 872-3228
www.colby.edu/museum

Outdoor Sculpture

• Skowhegan Indian, 1969 — Skowhegan
On High Street (Rt. 201) at the side of a parking lot behind the Cumberland Farms you will find this imposing figure made of white pine. Sculptor Bernard

Langlais (1921-1977) worked more than three years on the 62-foot tall figure. The idea came from Willard Cummings, an artist and a founder of Skowhegan School of Painting and Sculpture. The Skowhegan Tourist Hospitality Association commissioned the work and, in 1969, on the anniversary of Maine's 150th year as a state, it was dedicated to Maine's Native Americans. The figure holds both fishing weir and spear, looking to the Kennebec River where early Native Americans largely drew their sustenance. In time this amazing sculpture will be moved to a more prominent and appropriate location.

• Wall of Refuse (begun 1975) — Harmony

This is one for the books. Back in 1975, mixed media artist Wally Warren (b. 1945) began a found-art assemblage of, well, just about everything — creating a whimsical Wall of Refuse. The Wall is an enormous fence of painted objects that he has come across — the detritus of our use-and-throw-away society. Expect to find bottles, gas masks, bikes, ironing boards, bedsteads, wheels, electronics, etc. The never-ending growth of the Wall reflects our continuing consumption mentality. The Wall is located at Wally's former home and studio, off winding Rt. 154 about 10 miles west of Dexter.

Film

• Maine International Film Festival (MIFF) — Waterville

This is a very ambitious, one-week festival with more than 50 film offerings, shown in multiple locations. In the past, everything from On Golden Pond, to a very real documentary about the kids of gay and lesbian parents, to the lives of Scott and Helen Nearing of Good Life fame, to how the women of the 1976 Yale rowing team helped bring about equality in sports. Something for everyone who loves films.

Festival scheduled for July. Check for current offerings, dates, times and venues.
MIFF, 10 Railroad Square, Waterville, ME 04901
Tel: (207) 861-8138   Fax: (207) 872-5502
www.railroadsquarecinema.com/miff/
email: info@miff.org

Moosehead Lake & Katahdin

Outdoor Sculpture

• Enchanted Forest (1981) — three miles south of Dover-Foxcroft

Make sure your kids know about this one — so you'll have an excuse to see it yourself. This is a sculptural comic book with lovable characters. It all started back in 1981 when retired dairyman Ardell Flanders started clearing a white pine lot that had been ruined by insects. He began by clearing a path for his wife's walks, then, just to please her, he sculpted a unicorn. Her approval set him off on making an elephant. The neighborhood kids approved and then there was no stopping Ardell. Today in the sculptural playground you'll see Charlie Brown playing ball, Rip Van Winkle and his friends with bowling pins, Alice and the Mad Hatter at tea and a host of other characters and fun objects. It's all child-sized and hands on. Fun for the entire family.

Trains — Back in Time

Courtesy of Maine Narrow Guage Railroad & Museum, Portland

There was a day long ago when railroads were an essential part of the state's transportation system. There are few trains left, but the best of them are preserved in old narrow-gauge museums and railbeds scattered around the state. Here's where you can enjoy them.

Southern Coastal

• Seashore Trolley Museum — Kennebunkport
   Operating trolley museum.
Log Cabin Road, Drawer A, Kennebunkport, ME 04046-1690
(207) 967-2712
email: carshop@biddeford.com

• Great Northern Narrow Gauge Railroad — Biddeford
PO Box 661, Biddeford, ME 04005
(207) 282-9255

Greater Portland

• Maine Narrow Gauge Railroad and Museum — Portland
   Both steam and diesel trains on 1.5 miles of track through Portland Harbor and Casco Bay area past forts, lighthouses, islands, ships. A 1913 Vulcan and a 1924 Baldwin are featured along with a railbus, Model-T

inspection car and a Fairmont.
58 Fore Street, Portland, ME 04101
(207) 828-0814
http://mngrr.rails.net

Western Mountains & Lakes

• Sandy River Railroad Park — Phillips
    Two-foot narrow-gauge railroad.
PO Box B, Phillips, ME 04966
(207) 639-2881

Midcoast

• Belfast & Moosehead Lake Railroad — Unity
    Extra attraction is fine dining while seeing the beautiful countryside. Dinner and dinner/theater trains. You can even work on the railroad — including a stint as the engineer of the antique Swedish steam locomotive.
One Depot Square, Unity, ME 04988
1-800-392-5500
www.belfastrailroad.com

• Wiscasset, Waterville & Farmington Railway Museum — Alna
    Sheepscot Station, Alna, ME 04535
(207) 882-4193
aol instant messenger: WWandF Rwy
email: webmaster@wwfry.org

• Boothbay Railway Village — Boothbay
    Narrow-gauge coal-fired steam train in a re-created historic village. 50 antique vehicles on display.
PO Box 123, Boothbay, ME 04537
(207) 633-4727
www.railwayvillage.org
email: railvill@lincoln.midcoast.com

Down East

• Bucksport Historical Society Museum — Bucksport
   Railroad station containing items of local history.
Main Street, Bucksport, ME
(207) 469-2591

Far North

• Fort Fairfield Railroad Museum
   Depot museum located in former Bangor & Aroostook Railroad station.
PO Box 269, Fort Fairfield, ME
(207) 834-5248

• Oakfield Railroad Museum
   Photos, vintage signs and other railroad memorabilia. Restored caboose, motor car and a manually-propelled car.
PO Box 62, Oakfield, ME 04763
(207) 757-8575
email: oakfield.rr.museum@ainop.co

Index

Notes